I0436604

Canon EOS R7 Instructional Handbook

A User-friendly Guidebook Tailored to Assist EOS R7 Owners in Mastering their Camera's Features

By

Harry Bass

Table of Content

INTRODUCTION

People liked Canon's first EOS R-series cameras and RF lenses because they were small, advanced, and suitable for professionals, hobbyists, and beginners. Even people who used other camera brands were interested. Now, Canon has made the R-series even better by adding dual memory card slots and in-body image stabilization. They've also introduced two new smaller APS-C mirrorless cameras: the basic R10 and the advanced EOS R7, which this book is about.

The EOS R7 is part of the R-system, which is now a solid choice for those who want a full-frame camera (like EOS R3, R5, or R6) or an APS-C model. Canon offers many lenses for the camera's RF mount, and more are planned. You can also use existing EF-/EF-S-mount lenses with adapters, and there's a range of flash units and accessories compatible with both EF and RF cameras, making it a versatile system.

The Canon R-series cameras are not Canon's first mirrorless interchangeable-lens cameras. Canon previously had the EOS M line, smaller cameras aimed at casual users. The experience gained from those cameras helped design the new R-series, catering to dedicated photo enthusiasts and professionals.

You might wonder, "How do I use this camera?" The Canon manual is complicated, and those YouTube tutorials with ads must be explained more clearly. Who wants to learn by staring at a screen? Wouldn't you instead go out and take photos with your camera?

Canon's big manuals in PDF format have lots of information, but they need to explain why you should use specific settings. How they're organized makes it hard to find what you're looking for, and you must flip between different sections. The basic manual could be better too, with black-and-white drawings and small pictures that don't show off what you can do.

This guide helps you use your R7 camera to take any picture you like. Instead of telling you where to stand for specific shots, it teaches you how to choose the right settings like autofocus, shutter speed, f/stop, or flash for great sports photos.

CHAPTER 1: GETTING THE CAMERA UP AND RUNNING

Preparing the Camera for Initial Use

Setting up your camera is quick and straightforward. Just charge the battery, attach a lens, adjust the viewfinder, insert and format a memory card, and make a few settings. These steps are easy, especially if you know previous EOS models. I'll provide some extra details if you're new to Canon or digital SLR cameras.

Power Options

Your Canon EOS R7 is a fancy device; to make it work, you must charge its battery first. The LP-E6NH lithium-ion battery can give you around 380–770 shots when fully charged, depending on whether you use the screen or viewfinder. This estimate follows tests by the Camera & Imaging Products Association.

Rechargeable camera batteries gradually lose some power even when not in use. It is because of a chemical reaction in lithium-ion batteries, standard in cameras, that causes them to discharge slowly. If your camera's battery has been sitting around, it might have lost some charge, and it's a good idea to recharge it before you use the camera extensively.

There are different chargers for your camera, but most people prefer the compact LC-E6 charger. If you get an extra charger, it adds more features and gives you a backup to keep your camera powered while you replace the main charger. Having a spare charger for emergencies or when I need to charge multiple batteries simultaneously is useful. Here are your power options:

- **LC-E6:** This camera charger is easy to use and works with older models, too. It's small, has wall plug prongs, and you can connect it directly to a power strip or wall socket without a cord.

- **LC-E6E:** It works like the LC-E6. It charges one battery but needs a cord. It can be useful if your power outlet is hard to reach. You can plug in the cord and conveniently place the charger on your desk. The cord is regular and fits many chargers and devices, like my laptop's power supply. I bought several and kept them in different places so I could easily connect my camera, laptop, and other devices without reaching behind furniture. The cord doesn't use any power when not connected to a charger. Remember to disconnect the charger when you're not charging your batteries.

- **Car Battery Cable CBC-E6:** Use the Car Battery Cable CB-570 by plugging it into your car's lighter or accessory socket. This way, you can keep taking photos even in places without regular power outlets using your vehicle's battery.

- **USB Power Adapter PD-E1:** For around $140, you can buy an adapter that lets you charge LPE6NH camera batteries using a USB Type-C connection without taking them out of the camera. I've successfully used a cheaper third-party USB-C charger that follows the Power Delivery standard. This charger starts with 5V at 2A but can adjust to provide up to 20V at 5A if needed. Regular USB chargers I've tested didn't work and showed an error message. If you see this error, turn off the camera and take out the battery for a few minutes, and the message disappears. When your camera is switched off, it charges through USB. You'll see a green light in the lower-right corner, and once charging is done, the light goes off.

- **DC coupler DR-E6/AC-E6N AC adapter:** These gadgets help run your camera using electricity instead of a battery. The DR-E6, priced at about $50, has a fake battery for your camera that fits into the battery slot. It connects to the AC-E6N AC adapter, costing $100, supplying power to your camera through a door on the handgrip.

Studio photographers need a power source that stays on for a long because they take many pictures continuously. They use cords or radios to connect their camera and studio flash to power packs or AC power. Using an additional adapter is acceptable in a studio setup. The AC adapter can also be helpful when looking at pictures on a TV, recording video, or taking remote or time-lapse photos.

Charging the Battery

When you correctly put the battery in the charger, a light blinks. It blinks until the battery is halfway charged, then blinks differently until it's 75% charged, and in another way, until it's

90% charged, usually taking about 90 minutes. To be sure it's fully charged, leave it for an extra 60 minutes until the light turns steady green. Once charged, put the battery in the camera, and to remove it, press the white button.

Mounting a Lens

To keep your camera safe and prevent dust:

- Follow these simple steps for attaching a lens.

- If your camera doesn't have a lens, choose the one you want and slightly loosen the back cap without removing it.

- Store the lens upright in your camera bag for quick access, and by loosening the back cap, you can protect the lens until the last moment.

First, twist off the body cap by turning it towards the button that takes pictures. Remember to put the body cap on when there's no lens on the camera. It helps prevent dust from entering and landing on the camera's sensitive parts, like the sensor. The body cap shields the sensor from potential harm by avoiding things that might accidentally touch it, like your fingers.

Remove the body cap and the rear lens cap. Put the lens on the camera by aligning the red marks. Turn the lens until it's secure. Switch the lens to autofocus, turn on the stabilizer, twist it off if the lens hood is reversed, and put it on facing outward.

The lens hood helps protect the lens and reduces glare from outside light.

Adjusting Diopter Correction

If your eyesight isn't perfect, you can improve what you see through the camera. If you wear glasses but want to use the camera without them, adjust the diopter (a knob on the left of the viewfinder) until the view looks clear when the camera is on.

Setting the Time and Date

Using the camera for the first time might prompt you to set the time and date. Just do these steps:

1. Press the MENU button at the top-left back of the camera. Turn the Main Dial to find the Set-up 1 menu on the same page as the Format command.

2. Use the QCD to move down to Date/Time/Zone.

3. Press SET to access the Date/Time/Zone settings.

4. Use the QCD to choose what you want to change (month, day, year, etc.). Press SET to activate that part and adjust with the QCD. Press SET again to confirm.

5. Repeat for other values. You can change the date format and activate/deactivate Daylight Saving Time.

6. After changes, use QCD to select OK or Cancel. Press SET to confirm.

7. To finish, turn QCD to select OK (if satisfied) or Cancel (to go back without changes)—press SET.

8. After setting the date and time, press MENU to exit.

Exploring External Camera Features

Topside controls

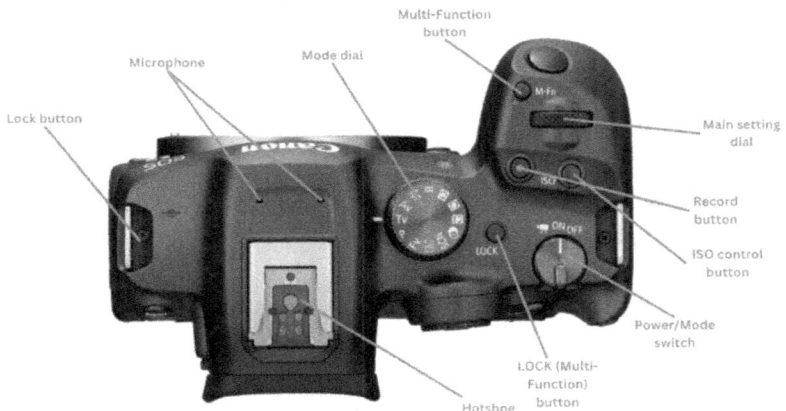

1. **Accessory Shoe:** Attaches extra flash or accessories.

2. **Microphone:** Has built-in stereo microphones.

3. **Mode Dial:** Turn this dial to choose how you want to take pictures.

4. **LOCK (Multi-Function) Button:** Stops accidental changes to settings when using the dials or lens controls.

5. **Record Button:** Press to start or stop recording a video.

6. **Multi-Function Button:** Press this button while turning the dial to adjust drive mode, autofocus, white balance, and flash settings.

7. **Picture Button:** Press halfway to focus and fully take a photo.

8. **Main Setting Dial:** Use this dial to choose shutter speed, aperture, and other options.

9. **ISO Control Button:** Adjusts the ISO setting.

10. **Power/Mode Dial:** Turns the camera on/off or switches to video mode.

Front features

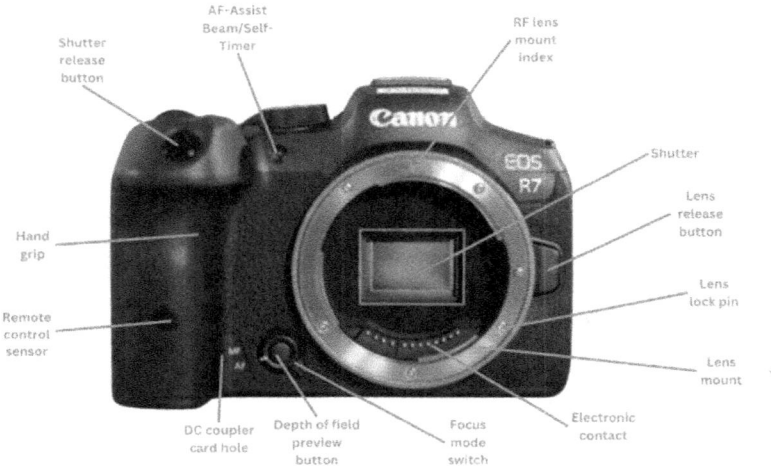

1. **AF-Assist Beam/Self-Timer:** This helps you see better in the dark and blinks when the timer is on.

2. **Lens Mounting Mark:** Line up the lens and camera when putting on a lens.

3. **Image Sensor:** A 32.5-megapixel sensor that captures photos.

4. **Lens Release Button:** Press to take off the lens.

5. **Microphone Terminal:** Plug in an external microphone (it's under a cover).

6. **HDMI Out Terminal:** Connect with an HDMI micro cable (under a cover).

7. **Remote Terminal:** Connect a wired remote (under a cover).

8. **Digital Terminal:** Connect to digital devices (under a cover).

9. **Headphone Terminal:** Plug in headphones (under a cover).

10. **Tripod Socket:** Screw in a standard tripod (at the bottom of the camera).

11. **Focus Mode Switch:** Switch between automatic and manual focus.

12. **Remote Control Sensor:** Used with a wireless camera remote.

13. **Memory Card Compartment:** Open to put in or take out memory cards (on the side of the camera).

Back-of-the-body controls

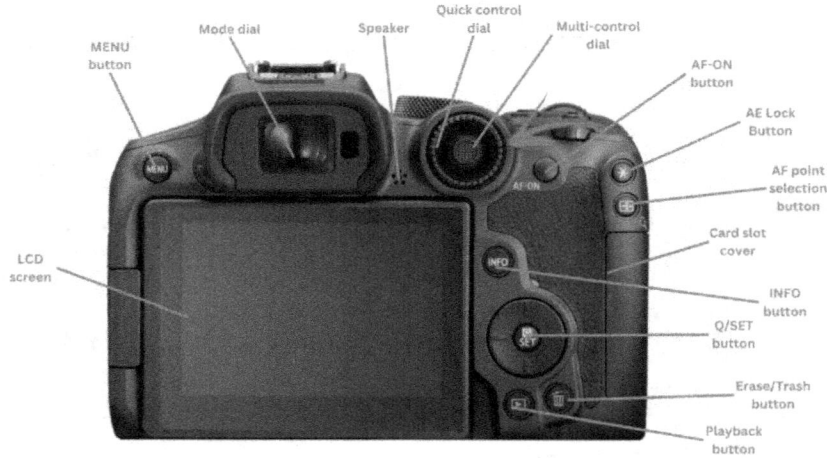

1. **MENU Button:** Press to open the menu.

2. **Diopter Adjustment:** Adjust this to make the viewfinder display clear for your eyes.

3. **Viewfinder Sensor:** When looking through the viewfinder, turn on the display.

4. **Speaker:** Built-in speaker.

5. **Multi-Controller:** Use for tasks like adjusting white balance, moving the autofocus point, and changing settings. Also, use it to pick menu options.

6. **Quick Control Dial:** Turn this dial to set exposure compensation, aperture in Manual mode, and more.

7. **AF Start (AF-ON) Button:** Press to start autofocus.

8. **AE Lock Button:** Locks the exposure.

9. **AF Point Selection Button:** Choose your desired autofocus (AF) point.

10. **INFO Button:** Press to switch between different information views.

11. **Quick Control (Q)/SET Button:** Press this to the Quick Control screen. Use SET to save a setting and go back to the previous screen.

12. **Cross Keys:** Use these to move around menus and make selections. The Trash key deletes the photo you're looking at.

13. **Trash Button:** Deletes the current photo you're viewing.

14. **Playback Button:** Press to see the most recent photo taken.

15. **Screen:** Shows various features and settings for taking and reviewing photos. You can touch the screen to change camera settings quickly.

Working with Memory Cards

Inserting a Memory Card

You need to put a memory card in your camera to take pictures. Please open the door on the right side by sliding it towards the back and insert one or two memory cards. Remember to do this when the camera is turned off, and it will remind you if the door is opened while it's saving photos to the card.

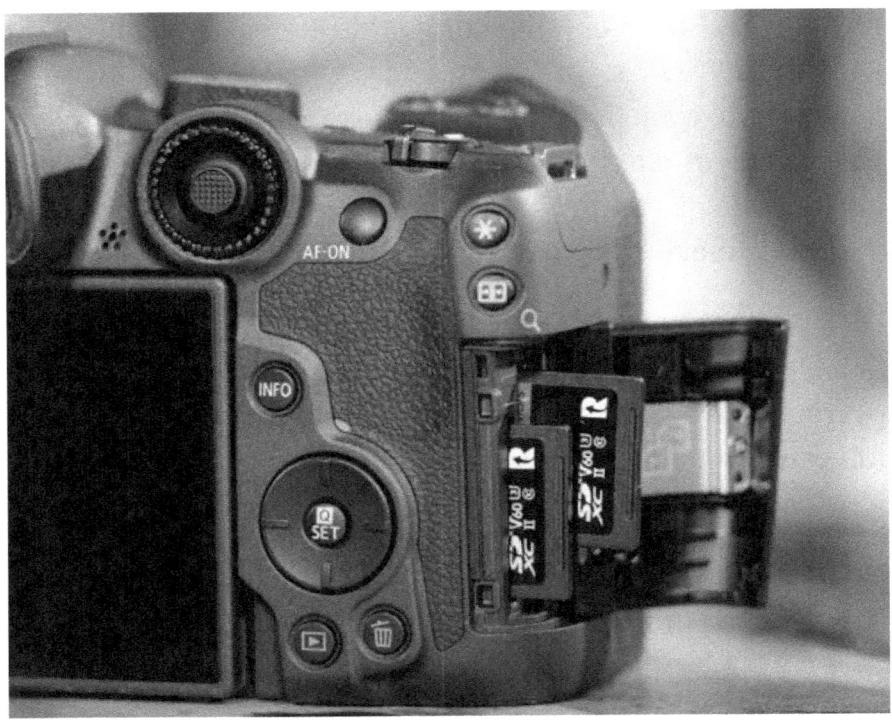

Put the memory card into one of the slots at the back of the camera. Ensure the label faces the back, and insert the edge with the contacts into the slot first. The slot closest to the back of the camera is Slot 1, and Slot 2 is behind it.

Both work with the fastest SD card type, UHS-II, reaching speeds up to 300Mbps. Note that various brands have different speed specs, including "X" factors and megabytes per second. Write speed is how fast the device saves an image, while read speed (often highlighted for being faster) is how quickly you can transfer the image to your computer via a fast connection like a USB 3.x card reader.

If you insert only one memory card, the camera will use it without any issues. In Chapter 14, I'll explain how to set a default card if you have two. Close the camera door to complete your preflight checklist. Remember to take off the lens cap before taking a picture! To remove a memory card later, press it down to make it pop out.

Using two memory cards in overflow mode is excellent for quickly changing cards when taking photos of breaking news or sports. For example, a photojournalist might replace a mostly full card with a new one to ensure they don't miss any crucial moments. However, I usually save my pictures on the main, faster, or larger memory card and think of the second slot as a backup.

Formatting a Memory Card

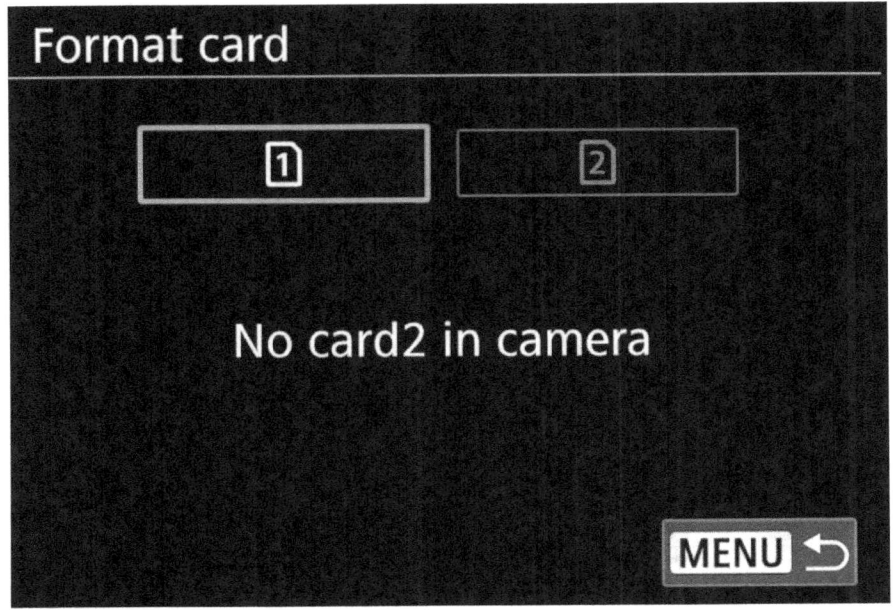

You can try out the new controls I showed you by setting up a memory card. There are three ways to make a blank memory card for your camera, but two must be corrected.

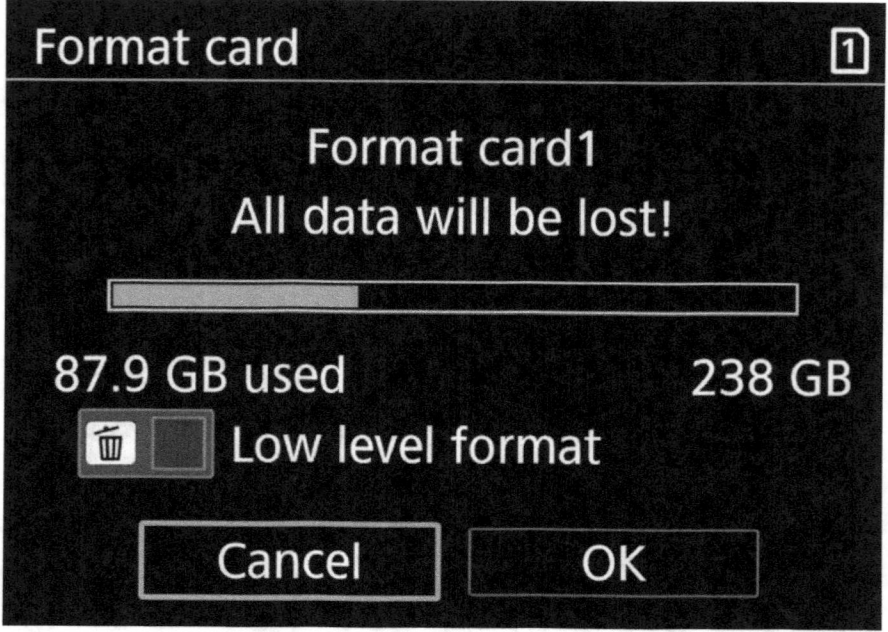

Here are the options, some are correct, and some are not:

- **Transfer (move) files to your computer.** When you move pictures from your camera to your computer, your memory card becomes empty. However, if you mark some pictures as "Protected," they won't be deleted. Also, this process doesn't fix issues with a corrupted card. It's better to format a clean card instead of just moving the pictures to ensure a clean card. You might not do this only when you want to keep some protected pictures on the card for a bit longer.

- **(Don't) Format in your computer.** To ensure your camera's memory card is set up correctly, don't use your computer to format it. Instead, use the camera for formatting unless the card is severely damaged; in this case, you can try letting the computer reformat it first and then use the camera.

- **Set up menu format.** To format a memory card correctly, follow these steps:

  1. Push the MENU button.

  2. Turn the Main Dial until you see the Set-up 1 menu with a wrench icon.

  3. Use the Quick Control Dial (QCD) on the back to move to Format Card in the Set-up 1 menu.

  4. Hit the SET button to confirm.

  5. Pick the card you want to format by turning the QCD and pressing SET to confirm.

Rotate the QCD to highlight OK, and press SET again to start the format. Press the Trash button first for a thorough format, mainly if the card has been used frequently.

CHAPTER 2: CONTROLLING FOCUS

Auto or Manual Focus

Better camera focusing makes photographers trust autofocus most of the time. The camera is excellent at determining what to focus on for regular things. Surprisingly, the shift to mirrorless cameras has made people interested in using manual focus again.

Creative photographers are using manual focus more nowadays for five main reasons.

- **WYSIWYG:** What you see on the camera screen is precisely what will be in focus when you take a picture. When you manually focus, you look at the same image the camera will capture. Some cameras use a mirror to show the image on a focusing screen, which might not be as clear or aligned as the final photo.

- **WYSIWYW:** Manually focusing means you can choose exactly what part of the picture you want to be clear. Unlike the camera, which might guess and focus on the closest thing, you have control over the precise focus, which is especially useful for things like close-up shots or portraits where you want a specific area to be sharp. The camera can't read your mind, so it might not always pick the right thing to focus on if you let it decide on its own.

- **Less confusion:** Canon improved autofocus, providing faster and more accurate systems with many options. The abundance of choices might be confusing for advanced photographers. If you find it overwhelming, switch to manual focus for more control and avoid concerns about when the camera focuses.

- **Focus aids:** Adjusting the focus yourself can make things look bigger on the camera screen. A cool feature called manual focus peaking, or "outline emphasis" by Canon, highlights the focused parts with colored outlines. The camera also has a "focus guide" to show how blurry the image is and which way to focus for a clear picture. I'll talk more about these options later.

- **More lenses:** The shorter space between the flange and the sensor makes it easy to use an adapter for various lenses, even ones not made by Canon. Some of these lenses are affordable and need manual focus, but they offer a broad selection. Many photographers used to autofocus find manual focusing worth it for the variety of lenses available.

How Focus Works

Focusing ensures the camera captures the parts of the subject we want to be sharp and clear. It happens automatically or by turning the focus ring on the lens ourselves. Manual focusing can be tricky because our eyes and brains don't remember to focus well, similar to how your eye doctor asks, "Is this clearer, or was it clearer before?" during a prescription test. Sometimes, they need to switch lenses several times due to subtle differences.

To manually focus, turn the focus ring until the picture looks clearest. Keep adjusting until you find the point where the edges of things in the image stand out the most.

Autofocus in cameras, like the one on your phone, checks how sharp the picture is. It remembers the changes well, making it faster and more accurate. However, what you want to focus on can sometimes be clarified. You need to decide that for good autofocus results.

Using autofocus is simple, but it's essential to understand how it works to get the most out of it. Once you get the hang of autofocus, you'll also know when using manual focus is a good idea.

The camera checks sensor data to see if the picture is in clear focus. It considers things like subject movement and predicts where the subject will be when the photo is taken. How quickly the camera can do this and adjust the lens for the clearest focus determines how fast the autofocus works. Your R7 camera usually focuses faster than your eyes, but in some situations, it might need to be quicker. For instance, the autofocus can be too busy when shooting a fast-paced sport with many players. In such cases, you can change autofocus modes or manually focus on a spot where you expect the action, like a goal line in soccer.

Autofocus works in two main ways: contrast detection and phase detection. Let's start with contrast detection, and later on, we'll dive into the details of phase detection in this chapter.

Contrast Detection

This mode is slower but can be more accurate, especially for still subjects. It was the original autofocus for DSLRs' mirrorless and live view/movie modes. Later, phase-detection pixels were added to the sensor, turning contrast detection into a fine-tuning option for a hybrid system. Understanding contrast detection will help you appreciate Canon's advanced PDAF system.

Finding contrast is like spotting the differences in a close-up picture of weathered wood. If the edges in the image have low contrast, they appear soft and blurry. The focus system doesn't care if the edges are horizontal, vertical, or diagonal – it just looks for the contrast between them, regardless of direction.

Take for instance a picture that is clear, with solid edges and noticeable contrast. This exaggerated example helps illustrate that a subject with high contrast is considered to be in sharp focus. While achieving focus with contrast detection is slower, it has advantages and disadvantages.

- Works with more image types. CDAF can be used with any topic that has boundaries.

- Focus on any point. Contrast detection lets you focus on any part of the picture without special sensors. You choose where to focus by picking a section of the image, and moving the focus around is simple.

- Potentially more accurate. Simply put, contrast detection in a camera is straightforward. It works well in good light, helping the camera find the best focus by looking for the highest contrast in the image. Sometimes, it may need a bit of adjusting, like overshooting and then correcting, but once it locks onto the perfect focus, it's usually very accurate. This method is excellent for refining focus achieved through phase detection autofocus (PDAF).

Phase Detection

The special pixels in the camera sensor split the light from different directions, creating two images, similar to surveying rangefinders or old cameras like the Leica M series work. When things are blurry, these images are apart, and as you focus, they come together to make the picture clear.

This method helps the camera know when the two images are perfectly aligned. Using phase detection, it figures out how blurry the image is and in which way (too close or too far) by measuring the displacement of a split image. It allows the camera to quickly and accurately focus the image and align the details.

The PDAF sensors are like tiny eyes that are best at focusing on things like vertical or angled lines. Imagine focusing on a wooden wall with vertical lines – easy, right? But it gets tricky for these sensors if you want to focus on something like the sky or horizontal lines. To make it easier, some sensors are designed to focus on vertical and horizontal lines using a cross pattern.

But, right now, putting special focusing pixels in the camera sensors takes a lot of work. Canon thinks that having many autofocus points increases the chances of finding details for focusing, even without those special pixels. The R7 camera's sensor has 651 focus zones and can use up to 5,915 positions for focusing.

In regular cameras, a pixel on the sensor can either focus or capture an image. However, Canon's Dual Pixel technology lets a pixel do both tasks, allowing more flexibility in placing focus detectors on the sensor.

Phase-detection autofocus works better when the distance between two images is larger, like measuring distances more accurately in trigonometry with greater separation between points. This accuracy is enhanced with wider lens openings (like f/2.8 or better) and may not work well with smaller openings below f/8. Comparisons can be done swiftly.

AF Pixel Layout

Due to the adaptable Dual Pixel technology, Canon can use autofocus over almost all of the up-and-down space in the camera frame and about 90% of the side-to-side area when using RF/RF-S lenses. Using EF lenses with an adapter might not cover the full frame; some could have only 80% side-to-side coverage, according to Canon.

The R7 mirrorless camera has a significant advantage because its phase-detect pixels cover a wide area, unlike traditional

DSLRs with fewer AF points. It means Canon's PDAF system on the R7 can now do things previously only possible with contrast-detection AF technology.

- Works with all image types. With lots of AF points on the sensor, it's unlikely for the camera to struggle with finding edges for sharp focus in the area it's looking at.

- Focus on any point. Contrast detection can check nearly any spot on the sensor. With many AF points, it can use almost any part of the sensor to focus. You can move the 1-Point AF point to almost any location you want.

- Just as accurate. Many PDAF points make it almost as accurate as contrast detection without searching and slow performance.

Dual Pixel CMOS AF

Knowing how contrast and phase detection work helps you understand Canon's Dual Pixel CMOS AF system, which is faster than traditional photo and video methods.

The camera's sensor has special pixels that help with autofocus. This system doesn't remove the image quality because it doesn't reduce the resolution. While it could have put autofocus sensors between the pixels, this would have left less space for capturing light. It's important to note that, unlike older CCD sensors, CMOS sensors have more built-in circuitry that also uses some space for gathering light.

Tiny lenses are put on top of each light-sensitive part to ensure light hits the sensor correctly. They fix the problem of light coming in at weird angles, especially with older film lenses. Newer digital lenses are better at getting light straight onto the sensor.

The Dual Pixel CMOS AF system uses pixels that do double duty by capturing both the image and autofocus data. Each pixel is split into two parts, working like separate autofocus sensors. An integrated circuit processes the autofocus data before sending it to the digital image processor, which combines the information from both parts to capture the full image.

Unlike traditional contrast detection, which often involves frustrating focus adjustments, Dual Pixel CMOS AF phase detection helps the camera focus smoothly, which is crucial for speed, especially when shooting movies where continuous adjustments might be recorded in the final footage. It improves autofocus tracking for capturing moving subjects in movies.

Dual Pixel RAW Focus Adjustments

The EOS R7 has a cool feature called Dual Pixel RAW. It lets you save special image files with extra focus info. You can tweak these files later to adjust focus, fix blurriness, and make other cool changes using Digital Photo Professional. Remember, this works only when using autofocus, and the regular image files won't have these editing options.

I focus on taking excellent pictures with the camera, not so much on using software like EOS Utility or Digital Photo Professional later. I'll briefly discuss the Dual Pixel RAW format's cool focus improvements in Digital Photo Pro. For more details, you can check the Digital Photo Professional PDF manual on Canon's website in your country.

Dual Pixel RAW is a special photo format twice the size of regular RAW. You can tweak it in some photo editing software (currently, only Digital Photo Pro can do this). This format lets you make small focus adjustments, enhance background blur, fix issues like ghosting and flare, and improve sharpness. Dual Pixel RAW saves two RAW files in one – taking twice as long – with info from all pixels (Sets A+B) in one part and only Set B pixels in the other. It can help advanced users recover extra details in bright areas.

To use Dual Pixel RAW, choose RAW or C RAW or RAW+JPEG/HEIF or C RAW+JPEG/HEIF for your photo quality. Then, turn on the dual-pixel feature in the Shooting 1 menu. Keep in mind that you can't use Dual Pixel RAW if you're taking multiple shots, using automatic HDR, the electronic shutter, or One-Touch image quality. Also, the two fastest continuous shooting speeds (H+ and H) won't be available.

We're mainly talking about adjusting the focus in simple terms. The DPR doesn't make your picture clearer, but it uses the camera sensor's information to help focus.

You can make tiny changes to where the camera focuses, just a few millimeters in front of or behind the original focus point. It is like what Lytro's light field photography did (look it up for more info), but on a smaller scale. So, if a portrait photo is focused on the eyelashes, you can adjust it to focus on the eyes instead.

Find Start Dual Pixel RAW Optimizer in the Tools menu of Digital Photo Pro. It looks like an icon that features an image area and tool palettes. There are four palettes; you can only use one (plus sharpness) at a time. Just check the box in the upper left of the palette you want to use for a specific image. Your choices are:

- Image Microadjustment. You can make things look bigger or smaller, from 100% to 400%, to see how the focus changes as you work. Use the zoom because the changes are tiny. A slider lets you move the focus closer or farther from your subject in steps of five. You can also choose how strong the change is, from 1 to 10. You can get a close-up of a Dual Pixel RAW image with the focus moved around.

- Bokeh Shift. You can move the blurry background or foreground to the left or right by values of 1 to 5. Just click the Select Area button and drag the area you want to adjust; the change will be subtle.

- Ghosting Reduction. Reduces unwanted shadows and glare caused by bright lights in your photos. You can choose where to fix it, but not how much. Dual Pixel RAW helps find and fix these issues effectively.

- Sharpness. This tool lets you make the picture clearer by adjusting sharpness. You can do this on its own or combine it with other effects. Like Canon's in-camera Picture Controls, you can control strength, fineness, and threshold, similar to other sharpening tools.

If you edit a Dual Pixel RAW file using DPP, the changes only apply to the saved file, not the original. You can experiment freely with this feature. Remember that the results may differ based on the lens, shooting conditions, and how you hold the camera (vertical or horizontal). Using the tool works best with a lens at its widest aperture, as changes in focus, bokeh, sharpness, and possible ghosting/flare are more noticeable in this setting.

Circles of Confusion and Focus

Having more things in focus is good. But when there's a lot in focus, it's harder for the camera to figure out what to focus on. It's like trying to focus in a dimly lit room – everything becomes a bit blurry and tricky to focus on, whether automatically or manually.

Using a lens with a longer zoom (200mm) makes focusing simpler than a shorter zoom (28mm) because the longer lens has less blur in the background. Similarly, a lens with a wide aperture (like f/1.8) is easier to focus than one with a smaller aperture (f/4) at the same zoom level because the smaller aperture creates more blur and a darker image, making it harder for autofocus systems to work well, especially when the aperture is smaller than f/5.6.

Taking pictures can be tricky because some things don't stay still. They might move in the photo, and even if you focus on one thing, it might change, or something else might get in the way. Sometimes, it's hard to focus on certain things, like plain walls or a clear sky, because they need more contrast for the camera or our eyes to focus properly.

If you need clarification about focus factors, don't worry; you're on the right track. Focus is measured using a circle of confusion. Imagine an ideal image of countless tiny points, like pinpoints of light in a dark room. When a point is out of focus, it turns from a sharp pinpoint to a small blurry disc with less contrast at its edges.

When a small blurry spot (circle of confusion) is tiny, our eye sees it as a point. But as it gets bigger, it becomes a blur instead of a sharp point, making that spot look out of focus. Enlarging an image on your computer or in a print makes these blurry spots bigger, too. A part of a picture that seems sharp in a small print might seem blurry in a larger one. Stepping back can make it look sharp again.

The size of fuzzy circles in a picture can differ for each person. People who see details well might think the circles are smaller than someone standing nearby. But usually, these differences are small. If a picture is blurry, most people will see it as blurry.

Only one part of your picture is clear, like a flat layer parallel to the camera. Everything in front of or behind that clear layer appears blurry, turning into a big blur that makes a not-so-nice textured white background less noticeable.

Looking at distant objects might seem like tiny points instead of blurry shapes. This is called depth-of-field. The range of these tiny points extends primarily behind the main focus point and less in front of it. This range increases when you use a smaller camera aperture.

Working with the AF System

Now that you know how the camera's focus works, let's explore the settings. To get clear and sharp photos, you must learn about focus modes (when to focus) and focus area selection (choosing what to focus on).

AF Operation

The focus modes in AF Operation tell the camera when to focus and how. They don't decide where to focus; other autofocus features do that. Focus modes determine if the camera should focus once when you press the shutter halfway or keep tracking and adjusting focus if your subject is moving.

◻	**AF**	▶	((ʏ))	⚊	⚘	★
1	2	3	4	5	6		

AF operation	ONE SHOT
AF area	AF⦗ ⦘
Subject tracking	●⁼ON
Subject to detect	People
Eye detection	Enable
Switching tracked subjects	1

The camera lets you focus manually, zoom in up to 10 times for precise manual focus, and has two autofocus modes: One-Shot AF (for still subjects) and Servo AF (for moving subjects). I'll explain these in more detail later. Picking the right autofocus mode and focus points is crucial for good photos. Using the wrong mode might make your pictures sharply focused on the wrong thing.

I made a mistake when I first took pictures of a baseball game using a camera that focused automatically (this was before digital cameras). I was taking photos of players on the field, but the pictures of a talented young pitcher turned out poorly. Instead of focusing on him, the camera focused on the fans in the stands behind him. I just realized this when I developed the film. The photos would have been better if I had manually adjusted the focus or used a different focusing method.

37

To save battery, the camera focuses when you press the shutter halfway. You have control over autofocus. Decide between One-Shot or Servo. In non-auto modes, press Q/SET, go to AF Operation, and toggle between One-Shot or Servo using the dial. Set the AF/M switch to AF before changing the autofocus mode.

One-Shot AF

In this mode, known as single autofocus, the camera focuses once and keeps that focus until you either take the picture or release the shutter button. It's great for still subjects, reducing blurry photos, but it may make capturing spontaneous moments slower. Remember that you can't take a picture while the camera is focusing. This mode uses less battery compared to other autofocus modes.

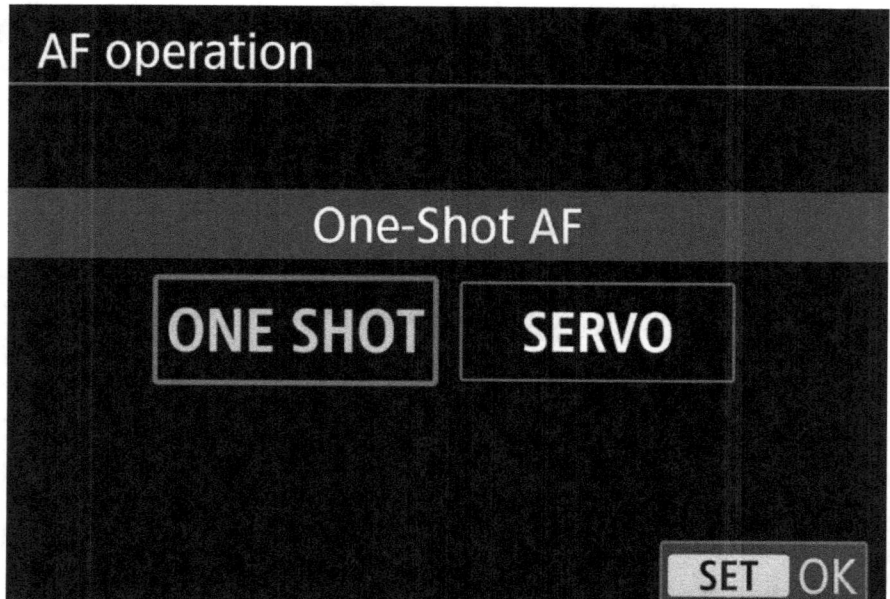

When the camera focuses sharply, the chosen point will flash green, and there will be a beep sound (unless you turn it off in the settings). If you're using Evaluative metering, the exposure will also lock. Holding the shutter button halfway lets you adjust the framing while keeping the focus and exposure set. While reframing, you can use the AE lock/FE lock button to keep the exposure based on the center point. If the camera can't focus, the point turns orange, and you can't take a picture even if you press the shutter fully.

One-Shot AF makes focusing quick and easy. You can just put the focus point in the center, aim at your subject, lock focus, and then move the subject to any position without needing to adjust the focus manually. It is speedy because you avoid the need to move the focus point yourself or rely on the camera to do it for you.

If you need to snap a picture quickly and don't have time to focus properly, you can change the setting in the camera menu. Instead of waiting for perfect focus, the camera will take the shot immediately when you press the shutter button, even if the focus isn't perfect.

Servo AF

This mode, called continuous autofocus, is excellent for sports and fast-moving subjects. When you press the shutter button halfway, it focuses on the chosen point but keeps tracking the subject. So, if the subject or you move, it adjusts the focus. The

AF point turns blue when the focus is locked, and there's no beep to avoid being disruptive during refocusing.

When you take a picture, focus and exposure only get finalized when you fully press the button. Servo AF has the least delay: press the button, and the camera takes the shot. It uses more battery since it keeps focusing when the button is partially pressed. In Scene Intelligent Auto mode, the camera switches to Servo AF if it sees movement.

Continuous autofocus, also called release-priority, means the camera takes a picture even if it's not perfectly focused when you fully press the shutter button. Servo AF, on the other hand, predicts and adjusts focus when the subject is moving towards or away from the camera, using either auto-selected or manually chosen focus points.

In simple terms, release-priority mode doesn't lead to many blurry photos. It just means the camera takes a picture, even if it's not sure the focus is perfect. Your photo could still turn out clear or at least close enough to being sharp.

Selecting AF Area

The Canon EOS R7 has 651 focus positions on its sensor to choose from to get the right focus. In Basic Zone modes, the camera picks the focus point automatically using face detection. You can let the camera pick or choose a specific focus point in other modes.

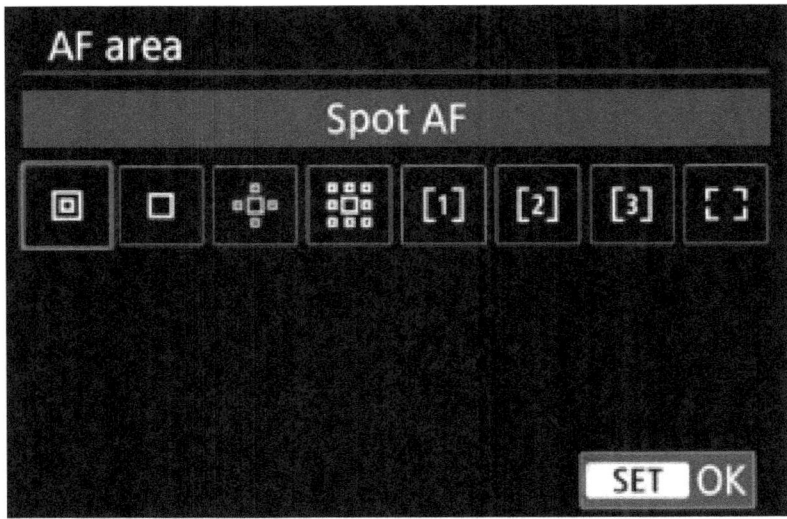

Your camera can choose or let you pick from eight ways to decide which focus point to use. Here they are:

- **Spot AF:** Let you pick a smaller focus point by hand.

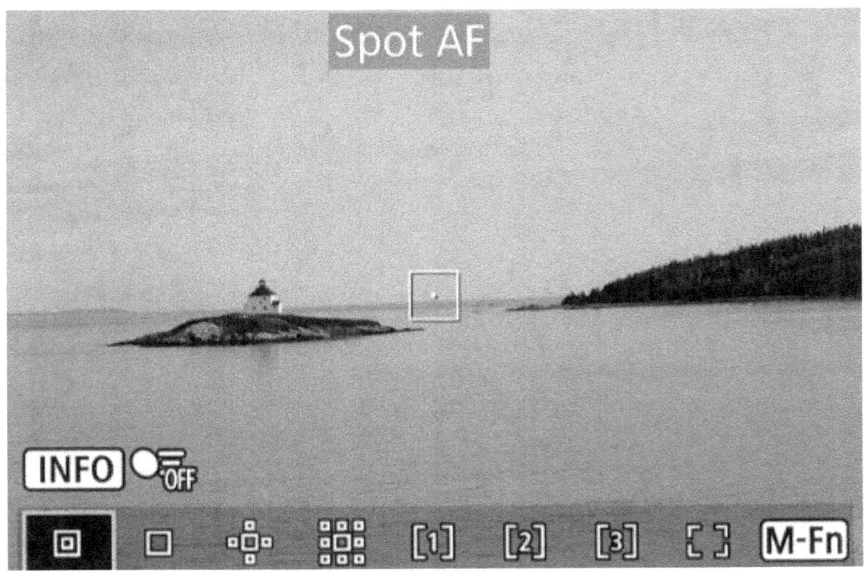

- **1-point AF:** Let you choose a bigger autofocus point, about three times larger than the Spot autofocus area, by yourself.

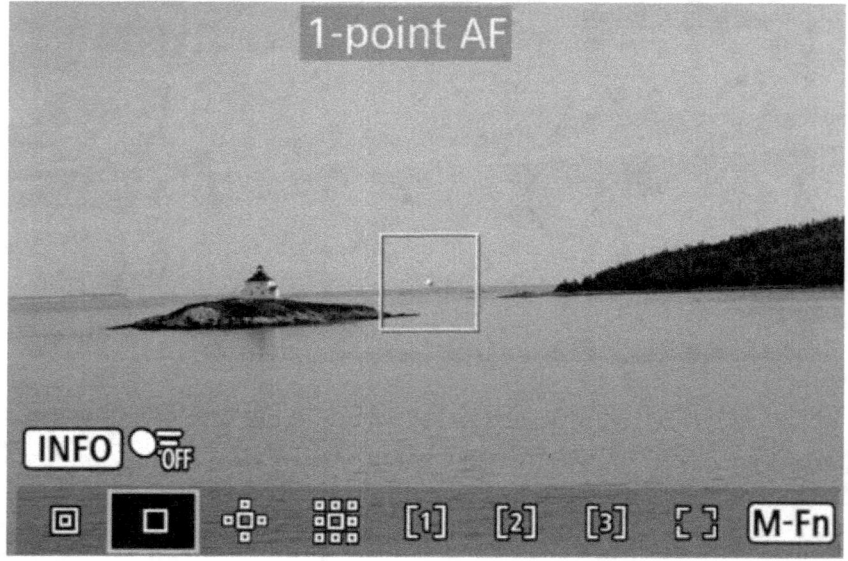

- **Expand AF area:** You can choose one focus point yourself or pick from the four points above, below, and to the sides of it.

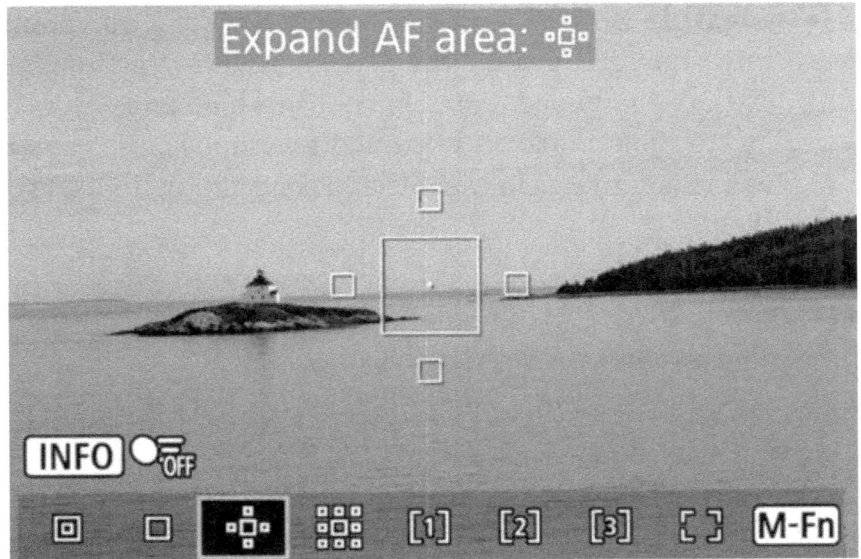

- **Expand AF area: Around:** You can choose one focus point or pick up to eight points around it in different directions.

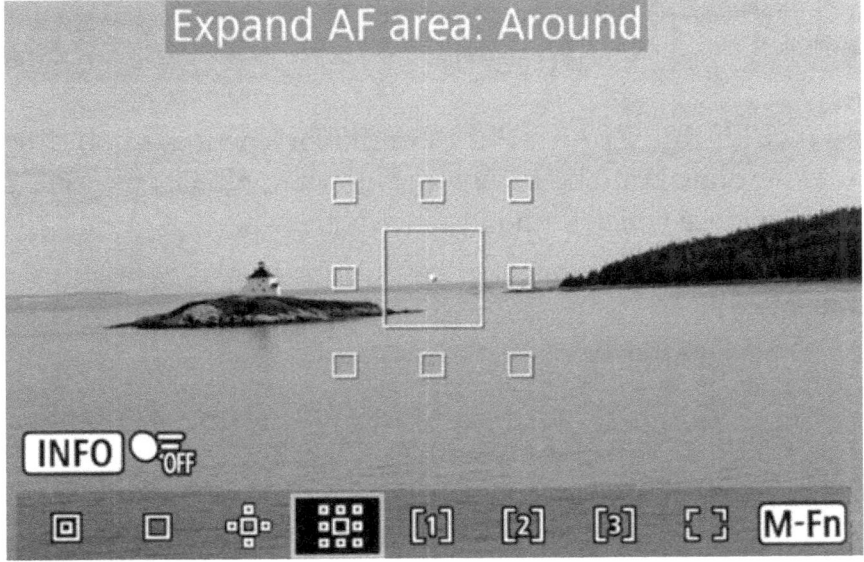

43

- **Flexible Zone AF 1:** The camera divides focus points into square zones on the screen, covering about one-sixth of the image. You can choose which zone to focus on. In Zone mode and the next two modes, the camera will look for faces in the selected zone and try to focus on them.

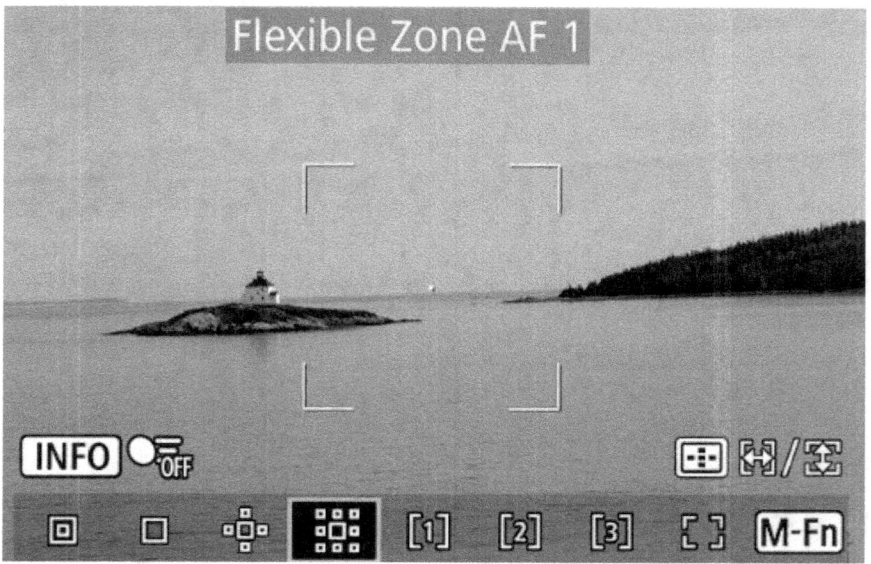

- **Flexible Zone AF 2 (Vertical):** The focus points are grouped into bigger up-and-down sections, and you can choose which section to focus on.

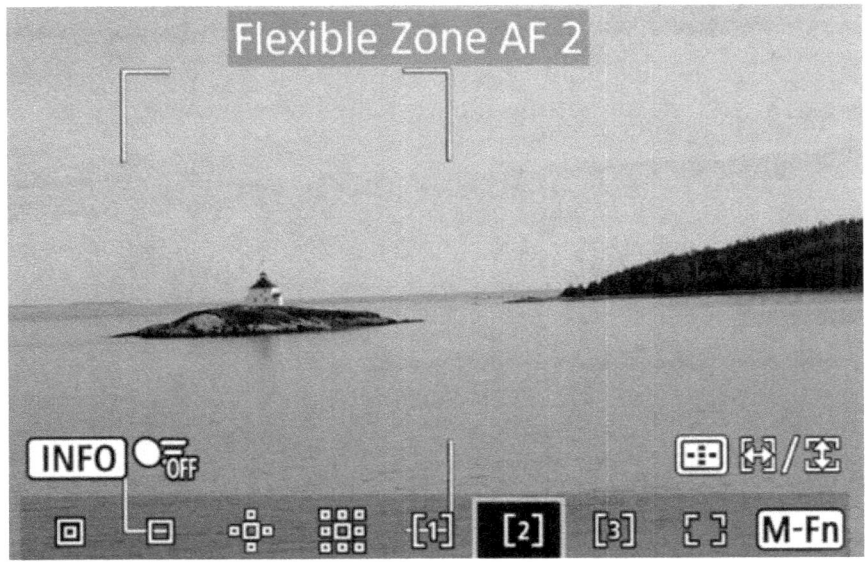

- **Flexible Zone AF 3 (Horizontal):** You can choose a bigger area side to side where the AF points are placed.

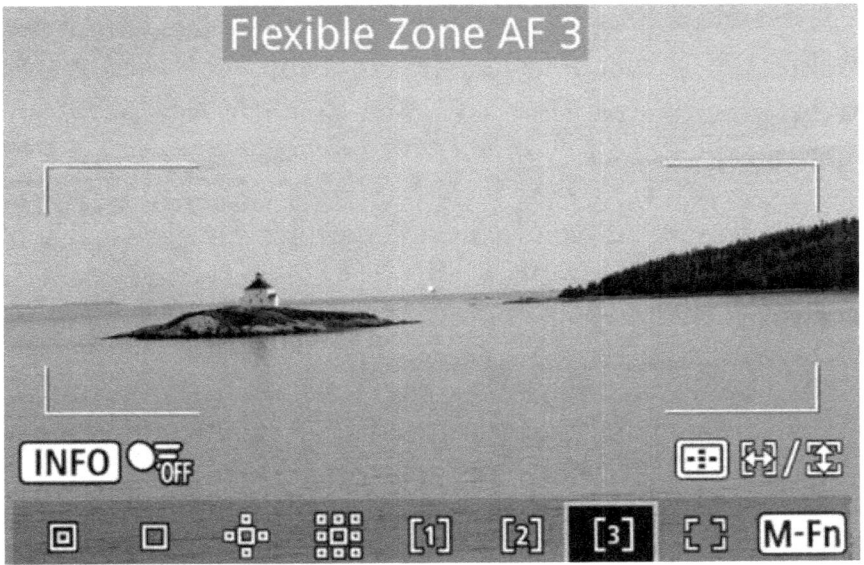

- **Whole Area AF:** The camera figures out where to focus by considering how far away the subject is and whether it's a person, animal, or vehicle moving.

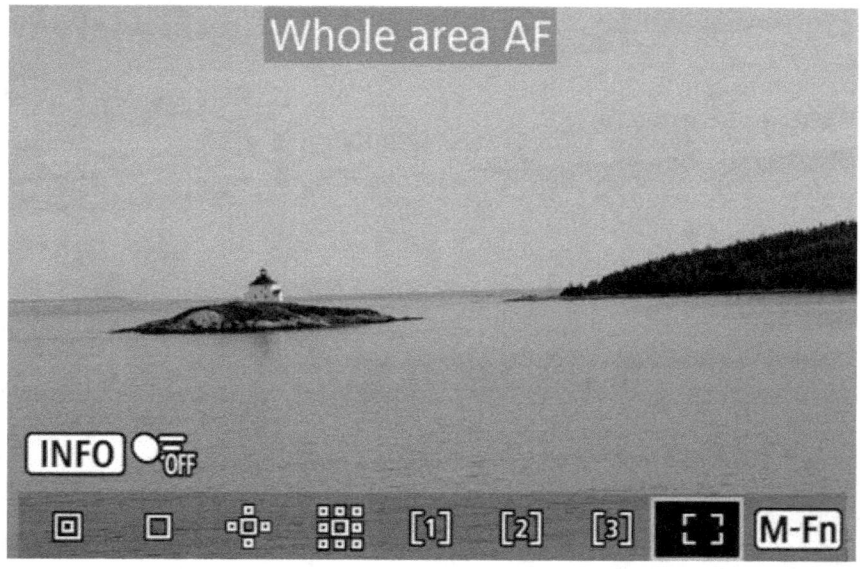

Besides the Quick Control menu, the R7 provides various ways to pick the AF area. Here's a simple guide on selecting where your camera focuses.

1. Press the AF point selection button on the back right of your camera to change the focus area. Do this whenever you want to pick a specific focus area or point.

2. Change modes quickly. After pressing the AF point selection button, press the M-Fn button on the camera within six seconds. Keep pressing it to switch between seven modes. You can also use dials or directional buttons.

46

3. Pick your focus area. While pressing the M-Fn button, the display will show focus area options. Use the INFO button to turn on/off Subject Tracking, and press SET to confirm your selection.

CHAPTER 3: PUTTING IT ALL TOGETHER

Taking a Picture

Gently press the shutter button halfway to focus on your chosen point. It also locks in the exposure based on your selected shooting mode.

Push the button down to take a picture. The shutter opens, a flash might go off, and the camera quickly stores the picture. You can keep taking more pictures until the camera needs a moment to catch up.

Shooting Scenarios

Capturing Portrait

Set your camera to Aperture Priority mode (Av) and choose the lowest aperture (like f/2.8 or f/4).

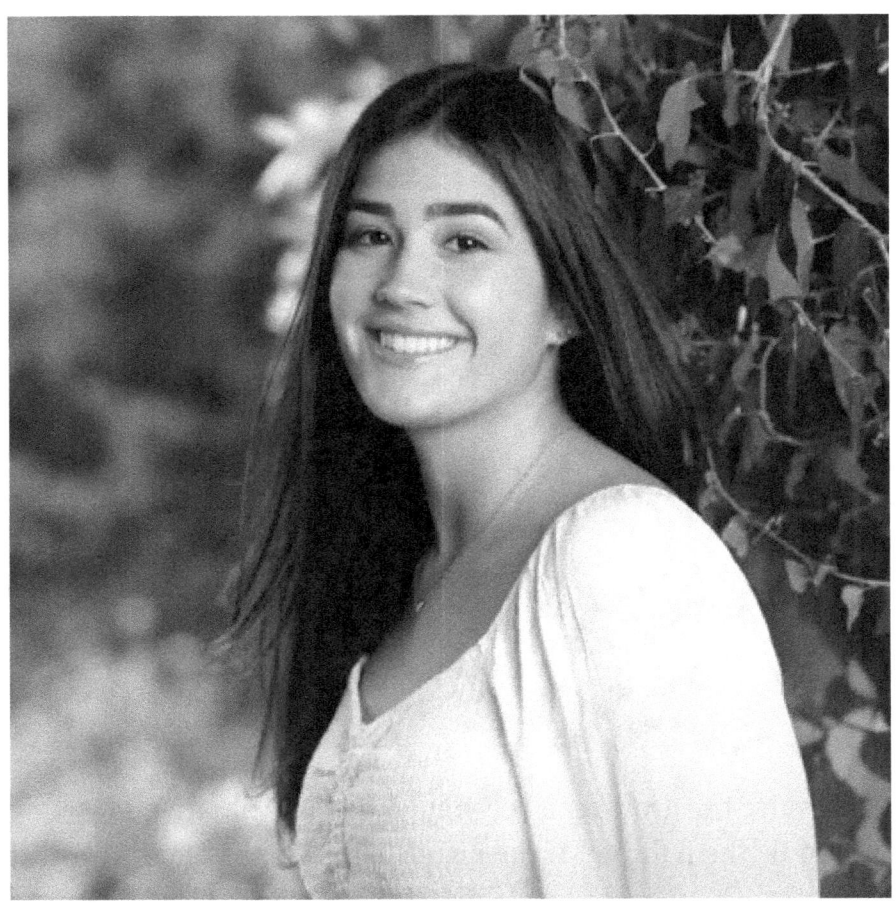

Focus on the eyes; if the photo is too dark or light, use Exposure Compensation to fix it. If it's blurry, increase ISO for a faster shutter speed. Use a focal length of 50mm or more to avoid distorting the face.

Capturing Group Portrait

To ensure everyone in your group photo looks clear, use Aperture Priority mode and set the aperture between f/8 and f/16. Focus on the person in the middle and check the LCD screen to see if everyone is in focus. If not, use a smaller aperture.

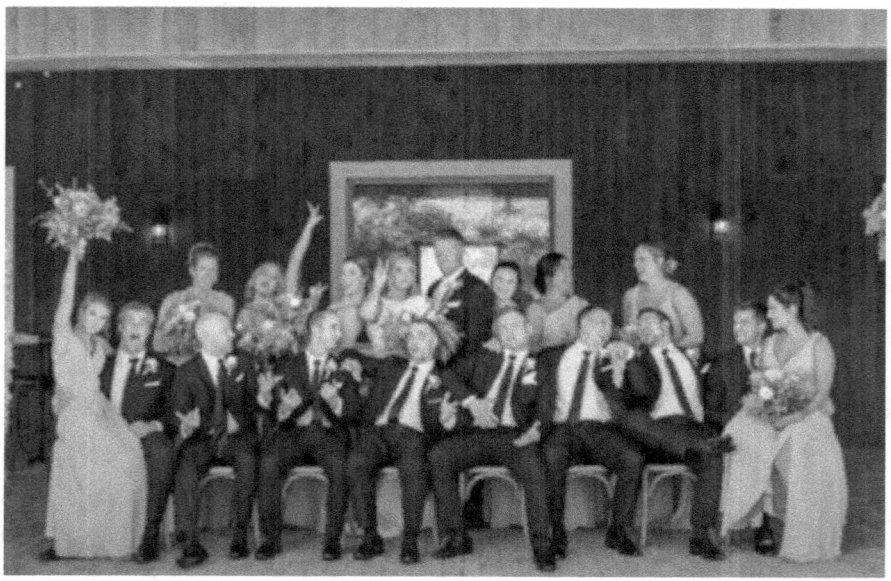

Make sure the group can see you, and use Evaluative Metering to handle the lighting. If the image is too bright or dark, adjust Exposure Compensation. If it's blurry, increase the ISO for a faster shutter speed.

Capturing Landscape

Take photos in Aperture Priority mode to control how much of your picture is in focus. Begin with an f/16 setting for a sharp overall focus.

Keep your camera steady using a tripod, and turn off image stabilization on a tripod.

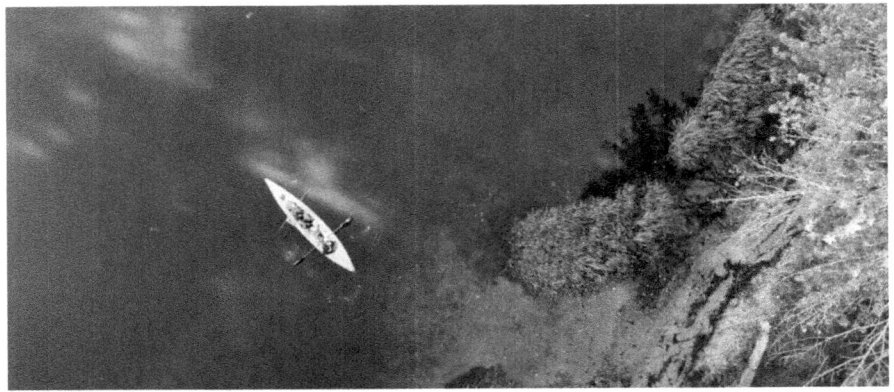

Choose Evaluative Metering and One-Shot Autofocus for better results.

Set the ISO to a low number (100-200) to prevent graininess in your photos.

Capture in RAW format for more editing options later.

Think about taking multiple shots with different exposures (bracketing).

Capturing Freeze Action

Use the SHUTTER PRIORITY mode and pick a shutter speed between 1/500–1/4000 sec to capture fast-moving subjects.

Choose SERVO autofocus for continuous focus on a moving subject.

If your photo is dark or blurry, increase ISO or try AUTO ISO for automatic adjustments.

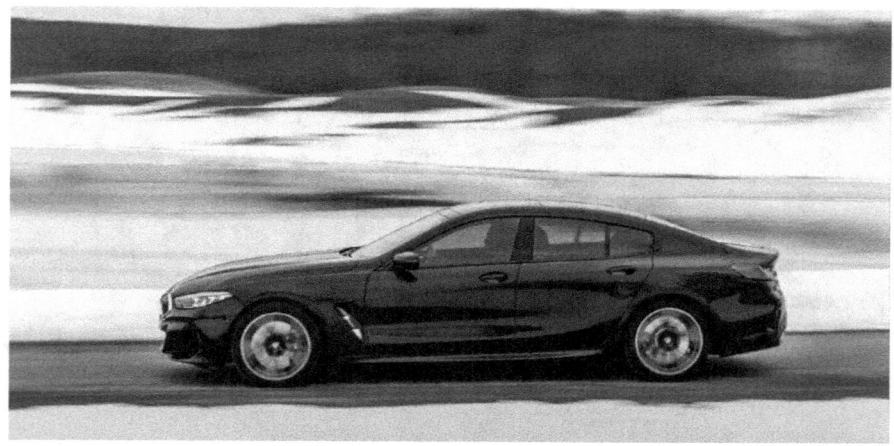

Capturing Showing Motion - Panning

Choose SHUTTER PRIORITY mode and set a slow shutter speed to capture movement. Track the subject as you take photos, and use SERVO autofocus with EXPAND AF AREA focus mode to keep the subject in focus.

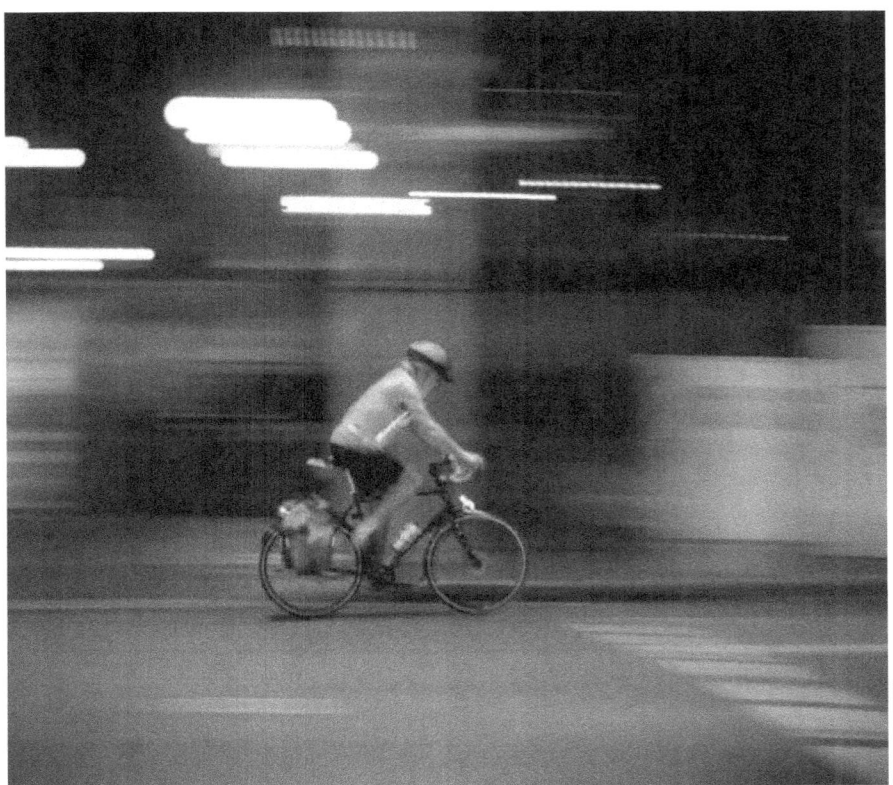

Capturing Low-light Action

Take photos in Aperture Priority mode and choose a wide aperture like f/2.8 or f/4.

Focus the camera on the subject's face using Partial Metering.

Use Servo autofocus with a single focus point.

Adjust the ISO to 1600 or higher based on the lighting conditions.

If the picture looks blurry, raise the ISO for a quicker shutter speed.

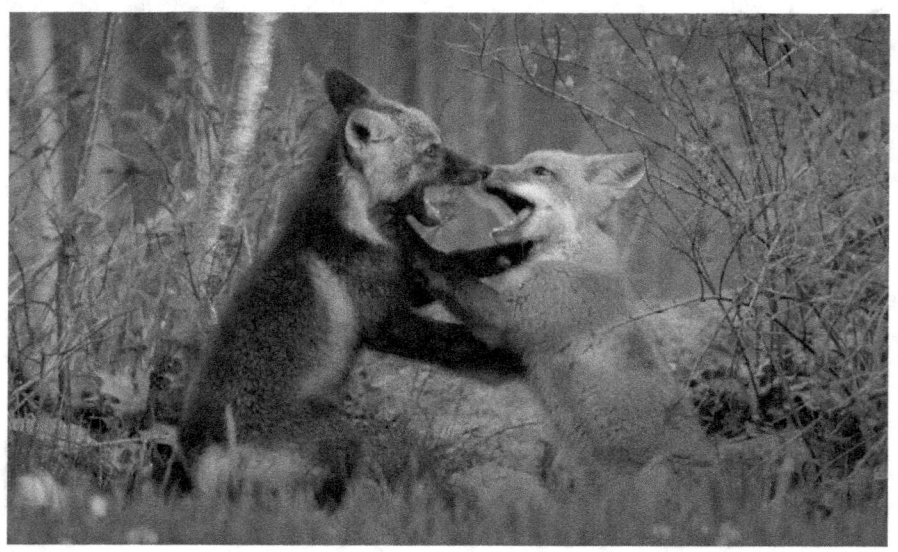

Capturing Long Exposure

Choose MANUAL or BULB shooting mode for a longer shutter speed.

Keep your camera steady with a tripod and turn off IMAGE STABILIZATION.

Opt for ONE-SHOT AF focus mode, or use manual focus if needed.

Set a low ISO (100–400) and shoot in RAW for top-quality files.

Prevent shaking using a cable release with a lock instead of touching the camera.

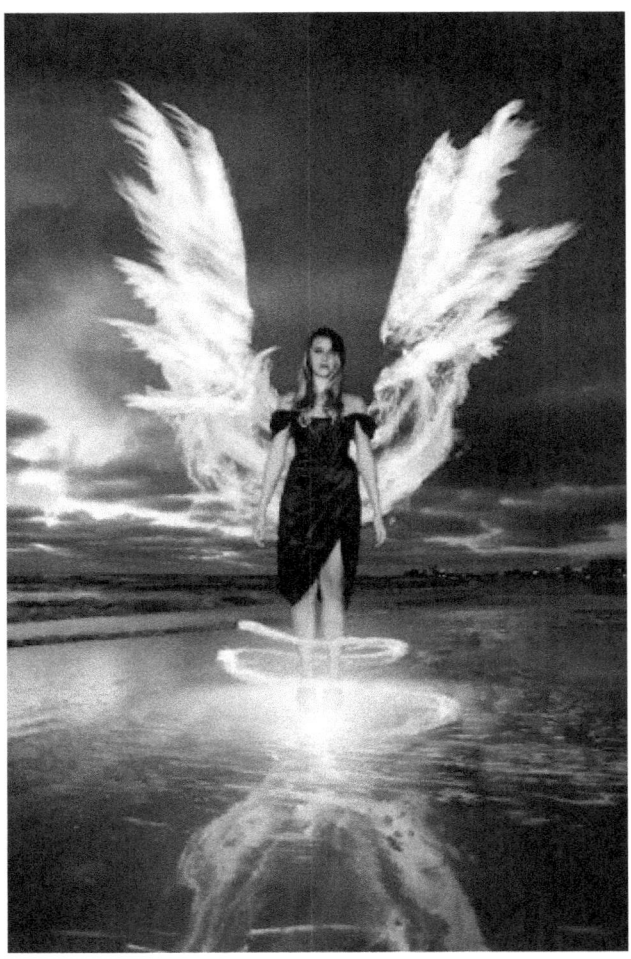

Capturing Macro/Close-up

Set your camera to APERTURE PRIORITY (Av) mode with a small aperture like f/13 for a clear photo.

Use EVALUATIVE METERING to check the light across the whole picture. Keep your camera steady with a tripod.

Use MANUAL FOCUS and Magnified View to ensure your focus is sharp.

If you're shooting up close, consider a macro lens or close-up filters for sharp focus on your subject.

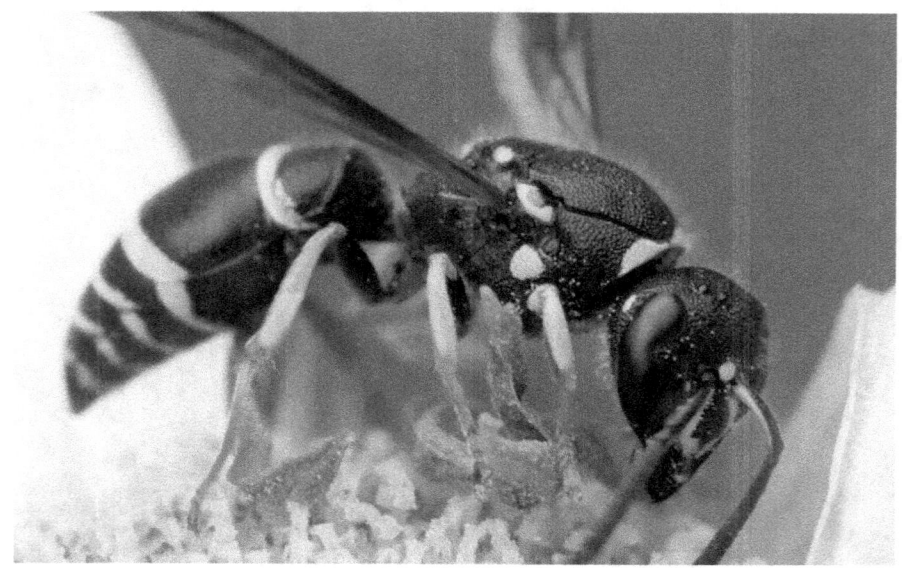

CHAPTER 4: CHOOSING BASIC PICTURE SETTINGS

Choosing a Metering Mode

Choose the metering mode next. Ensure your camera is in semi-automatic or manual mode, not Basic Zone modes like Scene Intelligent Auto. The default Evaluative metering is a good starting choice as you learn your camera.

To switch metering modes, go to the Quick Control screen. You can reach it in different ways, like using one of these three methods:

Option 1: While looking through the viewfinder:

1. Press the Q/SET button on your camera. It brings up the Quick Control screen for six seconds.

2. Turn the Quick Control Dial (QCD) to find the Metering Mode icon at the bottom left. Use the Main Dial to pick from the four modes.

3. Press SET to confirm your selection.

Option 2: While looking at the LCD screen:

The screen will show different pictures or information. To switch between them, press the INFO button.

If you see a picture preview, press the Q/SET button. Choose a metering mode from the LCD Quick Control screen. It's similar but you can tap choices on the touch screen instead of buttons. This is Option 1.

If you see the graphic screen, press the Q/SET button. Look for the Metering Mode icon at the bottom center, outlined in orange. Turn the Main Dial or Quick Control Dial to pick a metering mode, then press SET to confirm.

Option 3: When using touch controls:

Go to the Quick Control screen on either the LCD or graphics, as explained in Option 2. Touch the Metering Mode icon on the screen, choose the mode you want, and confirm by tapping the "Return" arrow icon to exit.

You'll use these four metering modes.

- **Evaluative metering:** The regular metering mode: the camera tries to figure out your picture and pick the right exposure by looking at many areas on the image sensor.

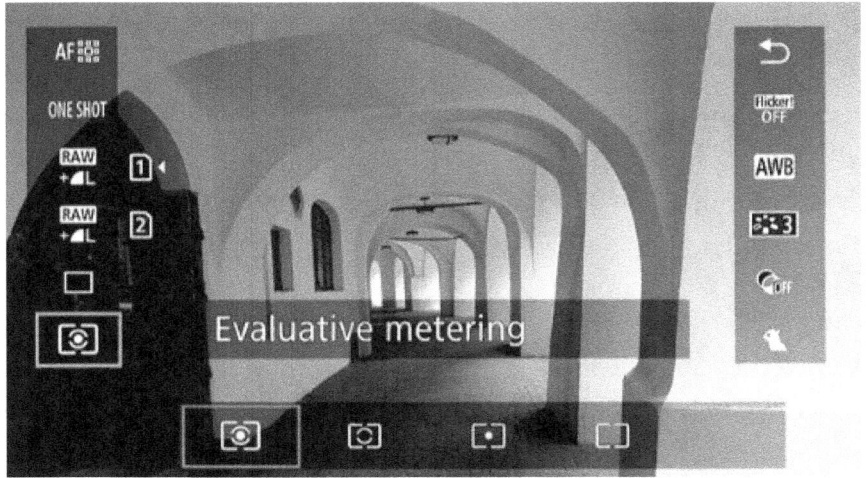

- **Partial metering:** Exposure is determined by a central spot that covers about 6 percent of the picture.

- **Spot metering:** The camera measures light from a small central spot in the middle of the picture, roughly 3 percent of the total image.

- **Center-weighted averaging metering:** The camera looks at everything but focuses more on the middle part of the picture.

Selecting a Shooting Mode

To start using your camera, make sure it's turned on, and if you've attached a lens, put in a new battery and memory card. Then, choose your shooting mode, metering mode, and focus mode. Turn the Mode Dial on top of the camera to pick your shooting mode. You can see the current mode in the viewfinder or on the LCD screen. Press the INFO button on the right of the LCD if you need to activate the display.

The camera has a super easy mode called Scene Intelligent Auto (A+ on the display) that does almost everything for you except pressing the shutter. It's part of Canon's Basic Zone choices, which also have Special Scene modes (SCN on the dial) and Creative Filters (shown as overlapping "filter" icons on the Mode Dial).

Your EOS R7 has six different settings to control how your photos look. These include modes like Flexible-priority, Program, Shutter-priority, Aperture-priority, Manual, and Bulb. You can also save your favorite camera settings in three custom modes, so you can easily switch to them when you want.

Aperture-Priority Mode

In Av mode, you pick how wide the camera's lens opens, and the camera decides how long to keep the shutter open. It is handy when you want a specific look in your photos. For instance, choose a small f/stop for a detailed close-up or a big f/stop to blur everything around your main subject. You could also set a certain f/stop that's not the widest to get the clearest shot with that lens or find a balance between speed and sharpness by using a particular f/stop.

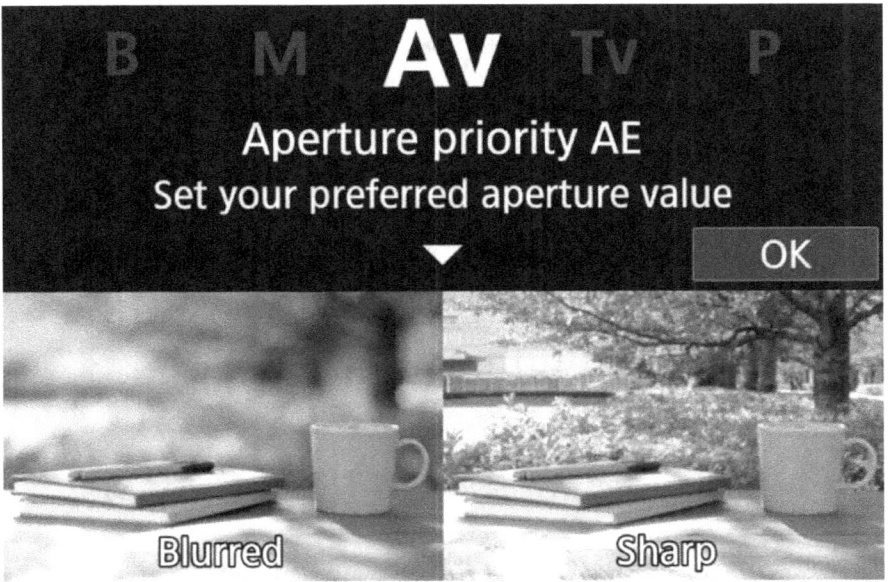

Choose Aperture-priority mode when shooting to set a specific range of shutter speeds based on changing light conditions. For example, if you're photographing a soccer game outdoors and prefer a high shutter speed but don't mind slight adjustments, set your camera to Av. Adjust the aperture until your desired shutter speed (e.g., 1/1000th second) is selected at your current ISO. Your camera will maintain that aperture (e.g., f/11) for depth of field, but it may adjust the shutter speed to 1/750th or 1/500th second if the lighting changes slightly.

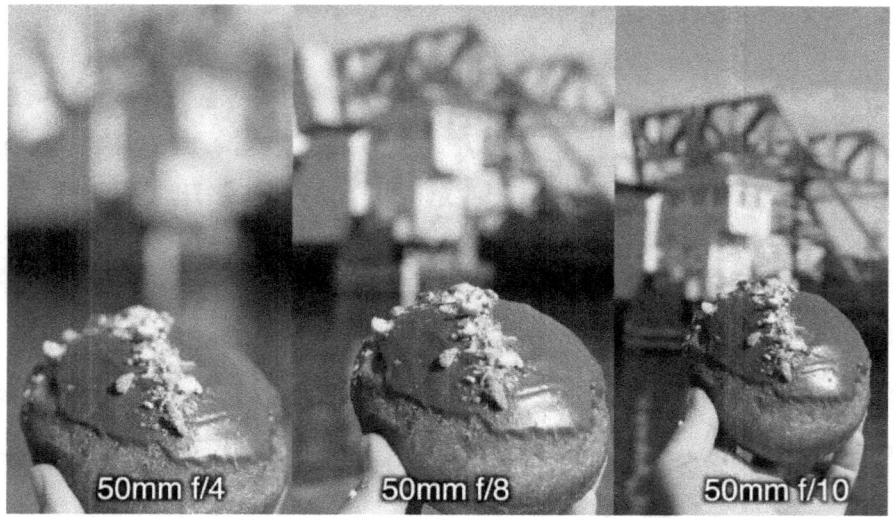

50mm f/4　　50mm f/8　　50mm f/10

If the blinking shutter speed on the screen means the camera can't find the right speed for the chosen aperture, you might get overexposed (if 8000 is blinking) or underexposed (if 30 is blinking) photos at the current ISO. To fix overexposure, pick a smaller aperture or lower ISO. For underexposure, go for a larger aperture or higher ISO.

Choosing an aperture setting that is too small or too large with Av mode can cause problems. If it's too bright and you pick a wide aperture like f/2.8, your camera's fastest shutter speed might not block enough light, leading to overexposure. On the other hand, in a dimly lit room, selecting f/8 might result in a slow shutter speed, causing blurriness due to subject movement or shaky hands.

Choose Aperture-priority if you're experienced with settings. Some experienced photographers always use Av mode. A Safety Shift feature automatically adjusts your chosen aperture if the

62

camera can't get the right exposure, even with flash. I'll guide you on setting it up. It works with P, Tv, and Fv modes too.

When should you use Aperture-priority mode:

- **General landscape photography:** Your R7 camera can capture detailed photos for big, beautiful prints or smaller ones with stunning details. To make sure your landscape is sharp from the front to the farthest point, use the Aperture-priority mode and choose an f-stop that gives maximum depth of field.

  If you choose Av mode and pick an aperture like f/11 or f/16, ensure the shutter speed is fast enough to prevent blurriness from shaky hands, or use a tripod. New landscape photographers often need to remember the wind-moving leaves and branches. For the sharpest photos, use Aperture-priority and increase ISO if needed for a faster shutter speed, whether holding the camera or using a tripod.

- **Specific landscape situations:** Choose Aperture-priority mode when you're okay with a slow shutter speed or want the camera to pick one. For instance, set your camera to Av mode, ISO 100, and a small f/stop when capturing waterfalls. It lets the camera choose a longer shutter speed to blur the water. You might even need a neutral-density filter for an even longer exposure. Aperture-priority mode is a good way to begin.

- **Portrait photography:** To make a portrait stand out, use a medium-large aperture like f/5.6 or f/8 with a longer lens (around 85mm–135mm). It blurs the background. If you have a very large aperture, like f/1.2, you can focus specifically on your subject's face. Even if parts like the far ear or hair are a bit blurry, it's fine if the eyes are sharp, especially in a three-quarters view.

- **When you want to ensure optimal sharpness:** Each lens works best at a particular aperture setting, usually a couple of stops down from fully open. This optimal setting varies based on the lens's maximum aperture. For example, my 85mm f/1.2 lens is sharp at f/1.2 but sharper at f/2.8 or f/4. When shooting with my 70-200mm f/2.8 lens, I use it wide open at concerts, but if I switch to f/4, I get better results. Aperture-priority mode helps me choose the best aperture for each lens.

- **Close-up/Macro photography:** When taking close-up pictures, the amount of the photo in focus is usually small. To control this, be careful with the aperture setting. You might use a small aperture for more focus or a larger one to highlight the main subject. Aperture-priority mode is handy for close-up shots, especially when the camera is on a tripod, and your subjects aren't moving much. In this case, a longer shutter speed is okay. So, choose Aperture-priority mode (Av mode) for better control.

Shutter-Priority Mode

Shutter-priority (Tv) is when you pick how fast or slow you want the camera's shutter to be, and then the camera automatically selects the right aperture (f/stop). It is useful for different situations, like choosing a fast shutter for action shots or a slow one to add blur for artistic effects, like in sports photos. It lets you decide how much your camera freezes or blurs the action in a given situation.

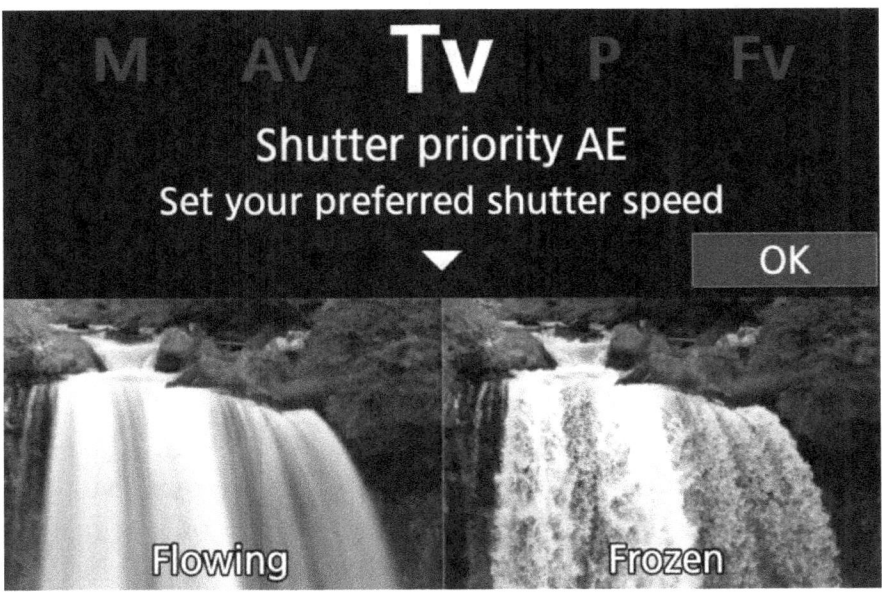

If you pick a shutter speed that's too fast or slow in Shutter-priority mode, you might face exposure issues, like a blinking warning, even when shooting outdoor soccer games on bright fall evenings.

If your camera's shutter speed is not right, your lens will blink to show under or overexposure. To fix it, choose a longer shutter speed or higher ISO for underexposure or a faster shutter speed or lower ISO for overexposure. You can also use Safety Shift.

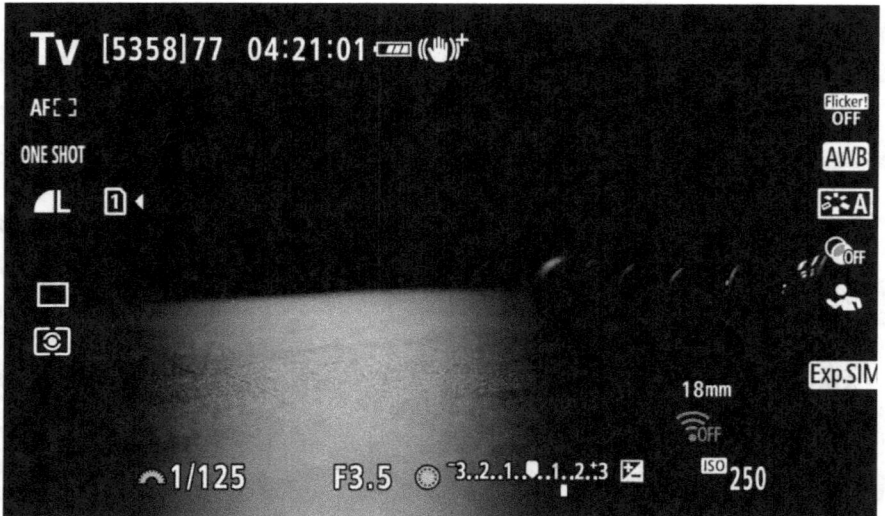

When should you use Shutter-priority mode:

- **To reduce blur from subject motion:** Make the camera's shutter speed faster to make moving subjects look less blurry. The right speed depends on how fast the subject is and how much blur you're okay with. For example, use 1/1000th second to capture a basketball player mid-dunk without blur, or go for 1/250th second to let the wheels of a motocross racer blur slightly for a sense of motion.

- **To add blur from subject motion:** Sometimes, you might want a thing to look blurry, like when taking pictures of waterfalls with the camera set to capture the movement for one or two seconds in Shutter-priority mode.

- **To add blur from camera motion when moving:** If you plan to take pictures of relay runners, try using

Shutter-priority mode and set the camera to 1/60th second. This way, when you follow the runners, the background will blur, but the athletes will still be in focus because the shutter speed is fast enough.

- **To reduce blur from camera motion when you are moving:** If the camera is moving, like when taking pictures from a moving train or car, and you want to avoid blurry photos caused by the camera's motion, using shutter-priority mode is a good idea.

- **Landscape photography hand-held:** If you can't use a tripod for your landscape photos, choose a fast shutter speed to avoid blurry pictures due to shaky hands. Also, set a high ISO so the camera picks the right aperture for clear focus.

- **Concerts stage performances:** I take pictures at concerts using my 70-200mm f/2.8 lens. To avoid blurry shots from hand-holding the camera and performer movement, I found that a shutter speed of 1/180th second works well with image stabilization. I use Shutter-priority mode, letting the camera choose an aperture in the f/4-5.6 range by setting the ISO accordingly.

Program AE Mode

In Program mode (P), the camera automatically picks the right settings for brightness and sharpness based on a database. If the picture is too dark or bright, the camera warns you, and you can adjust the sensitivity by changing the ISO.

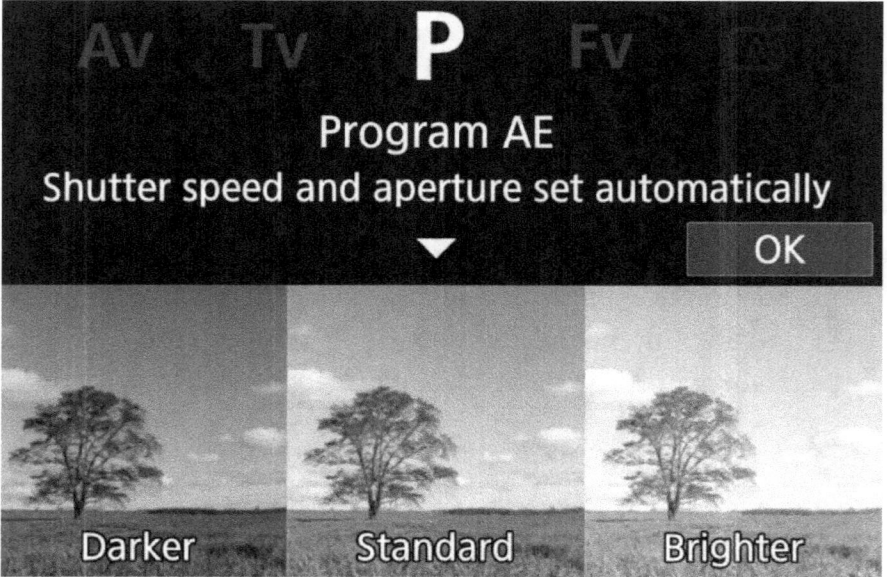

You can change how much light the camera lets in by adjusting the exposure settings. A feature called EV setting lets you add or remove exposure. You can switch to a different f/stop and shutter speed combination while maintaining the same exposure.

To do this:

1. Press the shutter button halfway to keep the current exposure settings, or use the AE lock button on the back of the camera to lock the exposure (look for the * indicator in the viewfinder).

2. The shutter speed and aperture display will blink if the camera can't determine the right exposure.

- **Underexposure:** If the number 30 on the shutter speed shows up blinking and the lens is set to its widest opening, you might need to adjust. Depending on the lens, the specific number could be different. To fix this, increase the ISO or add more light, like using a flash.

- **Overexposure:** If the 8000 shutter speed blinks, and you see the smallest f/stop like f/16, f/22, or f/32, adjust by lowering the ISO. A bright scene must be overexposed at 1/16000th second and ISO 50. For extreme cases like photographing a blast furnace, use a neutral-density filter or reduce light. After setting exposure, turn the Main Dial left for a longer shutter speed/smaller aperture or right for a faster shutter speed/larger aperture. This change applies to one photo; repeat the steps for the next.

Flexible-Priority Mode

Flexible-priority (Fv) might feel unfamiliar initially, especially if you're used to modes like P, TV, AV, and Manual. However, once you get the hang of it, you'll realize that Fv is intuitive. It combines all four modes, allowing full control over exposure settings in one place.

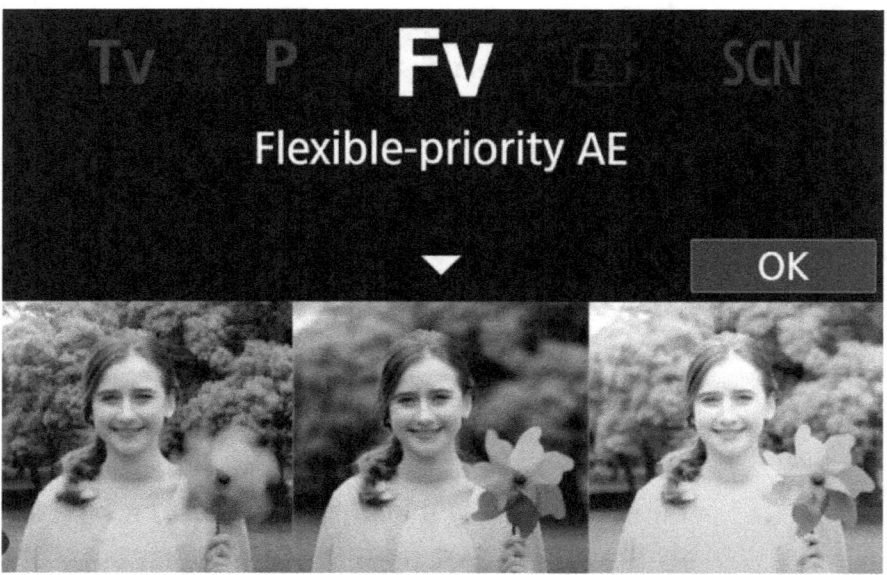

By default, it acts like Program AE with Auto ISO, but you can manually adjust shutter speed, aperture, and ISO, seamlessly switching between Av, Tv, and Manual modes.

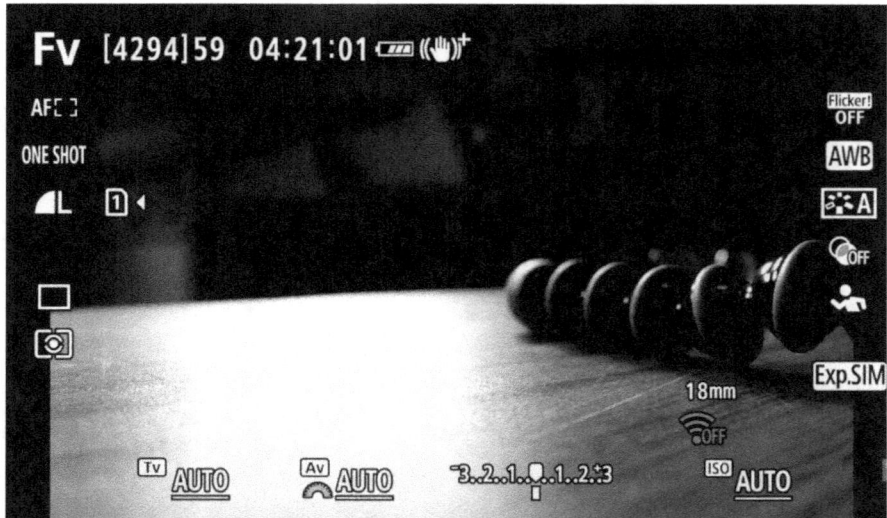

When Fv mode is selected:

- **Tv mode:** In Fv mode, turn the Quick Control Dial until you see an orange icon for the Main Dial next to the shutter speed. Now, you can use the Main Dial to pick the shutter speed manually while the camera adjusts the aperture and ISO automatically. It's like having Tv mode with Auto ISO.

- **Av mode:** In Fv mode, turn the Quick Control Dial until you see an orange icon by the aperture, then use the Main Dial to pick the f/stop. The camera acts similarly to Av mode with Auto ISO.

- **Manual mode:** In Fv mode, turn the Quick Control Dial to pick your preferred shutter speed and aperture. It makes the camera act in Manual mode for those settings while the aperture and ISO adjust automatically, giving you a Tv mode with Auto ISO.

- **Fixed ISO:** To turn off Auto ISO in Fv mode, turn the Quick Control Dial until the ISO icon is selected, then pick the specific ISO value you want.

- **Exposure compensation:** Turn the Quick Control Dial to select the exposure scale on the screen, then use the Main Dial to make the picture brighter or darker.

Manual Exposure Mode

To be a skilled photographer, it's important to know when to let your camera do its thing automatically, like using Scene Intelligent Auto or P mode. You might also use semi-automatic settings, such as Tv or Av. Sometimes, taking control and setting the exposure manually (using M) is best. Some photographers usually do this, relying on the camera's metering system to guide them using the exposure scale at the bottom of the display.

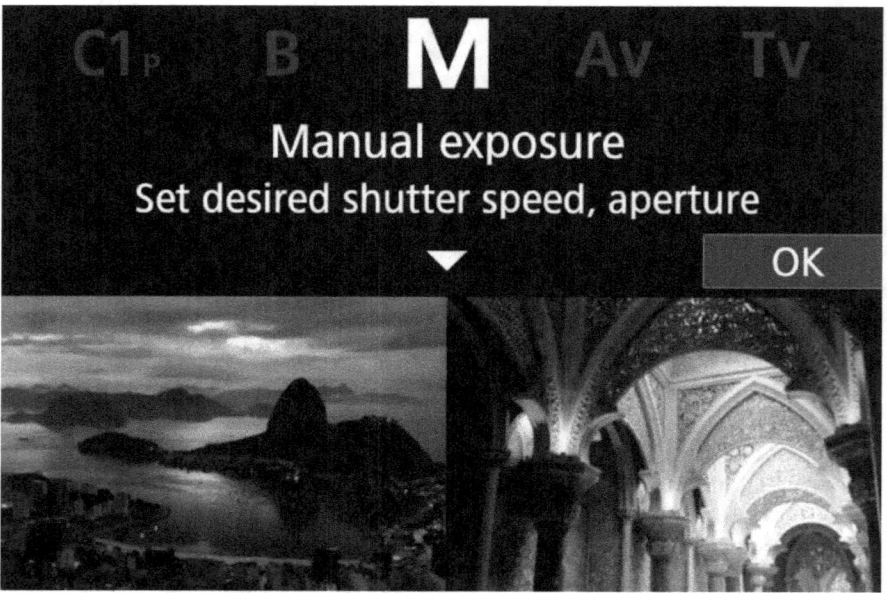

Sometimes, using manual exposure is useful. Imagine you're taking a picture with a dark background and a lit curtain to the side. The usual camera settings might not capture it the way you want. Even with special modes, I couldn't get the right shot of a ballet dancer against this backdrop. That's when manual exposure comes in handy—it lets you control the camera settings precisely to achieve the desired effect.

I took some practice shots, adjusting the camera settings like shutter speed and f-stop. If you're in a studio with multiple flashes, they're activated by other devices. Your camera's meter doesn't adjust for the extra light, so you must manually set the aperture.

If you don't manually adjust the exposure on your camera, that's okay, but it's essential to know how it works. Luckily, setting exposure manually is simple. Just turn the Mode Dial to Manual, adjust the shutter speed with the Main Dial, and tweak the aperture with the QCD. Half-press the shutter release or use the AE lock button to see how your settings differ from the metered exposure.

If you enable ISO Auto, you can fine-tune exposure with exposure compensation. Tap the exposure scale on the touchscreen, use the Quick Control screen, or navigate to Exposure Compensation/AEB in the Shooting 2 menu.

When should you use manual exposure?

- **When working in the studio:** You have full control of the lighting and can set the camera exposure yourself. Avoid letting the camera make its adjustments using manual mode (M). You decide the shutter speed, aperture, and ISO settings if you don't use ISO-Auto.

- **When using non-dedicated flash:** If you're using a flash that's not directly compatible with your camera, like a studio flash connected via a PC/X adapter, the camera doesn't automatically know how strong the flash is. In this case, you must set the aperture and shutter speed yourself.

- **If you're using a hand-held light meter:** To find the right camera settings when using flash or continuous lighting, use a handheld light meter, flash meter, or combo meter that measures both types of light. You can measure highlights, shadows, backgrounds, or other subjects individually with an external meter and adjust your camera settings in Manual mode.

- **When you want to outsmart the metering system:** Your camera's metering system is designed to handle different lighting conditions, like strong backlight, bright scenes, or low-light situations. It usually fixes these issues to give you a good-looking picture. However, if you want something different, manual exposure lets you create silhouettes, brighten up everything for a glowing effect, or intentionally darken the photo for a moody, mysterious look.

Setting Resolution and File Type (The Image Quality Setting)

Image Quality setting

This is the first option in the Shooting 1 menu. Here, you pick how well you want your pictures to be saved.

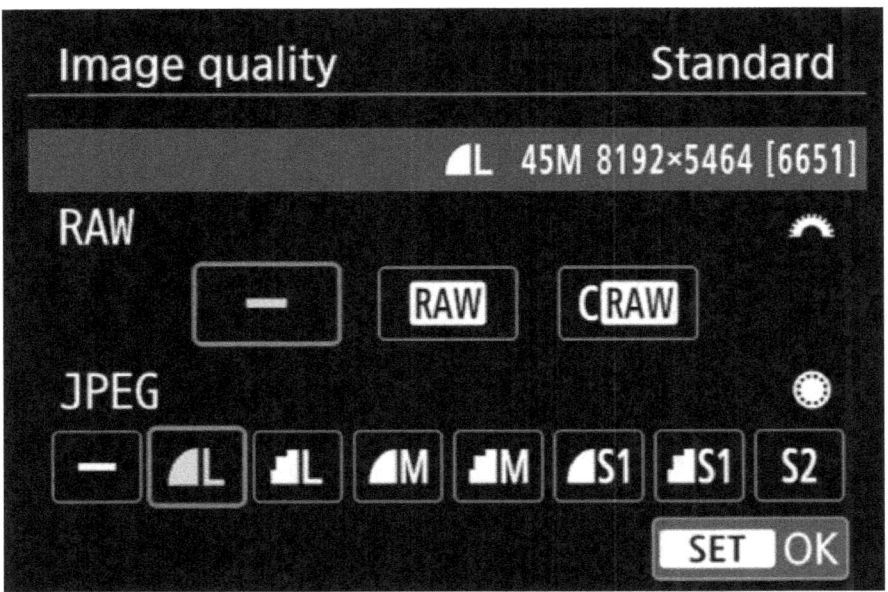

You get to decide the quality setting by choosing from different options.

- **Resolution:** The sharpness of your photos depends on how many tiny dots, called pixels, the camera captures. The options for the picture shape, like wide or square, include: Big and detailed – 6960 × 4640 dots (32.5 million pixels); Medium – 4800 × 3200 dots (15.4 million pixels); Small but clear – 3472 × 2320 dots (8.1 million pixels); Tiny but okay – 2400 × 1600 dots (3.8 million pixels).

- **JPEG/HEIF compression:** To fit more photos on your memory card, the camera makes your image files smaller using compression. It makes the pictures a bit less sharp, and you can choose between "Fine" for smoother results (shown with a quarter-circle symbol) or "Normal" for slightly jagged images (indicated by a stair-step icon). The "Small 2 (S2)" option doesn't have an icon but maintains a fine quality. I'll talk about JPEG and HEIF in the next part.

- **JPEG/HEIF, RAW, or both:** You can save your photos in two ways. First, as compressed JPEG or HEIF files that take less space. Second, as uncompressed, high-quality RAW files, which use more memory. Some photographers prefer saving a JPEG/HEIF for immediate use and a RAW file for later editing. This results in two versions of the same photo: one with a JPG extension and another with CR3, indicating it's a Canon RAW file.

To pick the settings you want for your images, go to the menus, find Image Quality, and press the Q/SET button. A screen will show up with two rows of options. (If HDR recording is on in Shooting 2, HEIF will replace JPEG in the lower row.)

Turn the Main Dial to choose from — (no RAW), RAW, or C RAW. Use the QCD to pick one of the JPEG/HEIF options: — (no JPEG/HEIF), Large, Medium, or Small in Fine or Normal compression (smooth and stepped icons, respectively), plus Small 2 (with Fine compression), at the resolutions listed above. A red box highlights your choice. If you choose — both RAW and JPEG/HEIF, then JPEG/HEIF Fine will be used once you've selected; press Q/SET to confirm.

Understanding file type

HEIF vs. JPEG

If you use an iPhone sparingly or explore its features, you might not be familiar with the newer HEIF format. Apple's iOS 11 introduced this format, and Canon was the first camera company to support it.

HEIF images are super-compressed pictures that look good and can be much smaller than regular JPEGs. They have extra cool stuff like transparency and richer colors. With HEIF, you can choose if you want super sharp images with larger file sizes or smaller ones that still look good but are not as sharp. It's an improvement over what we've been doing with JPEGs for years.

The problem is that no web browser can use it by default right now, and many programs and systems like Windows and Android need updates to handle HEIF. If you have a Mac, it needs macOS High Sierra or a newer version to understand HEIF pictures. If you use a recent iPhone with HEIF, it can turn your images into JPEG when you share them, but it still uses HEIF for special features like Live images.

HEIF (High-Efficiency Image Format) is a new image format expected to replace the older JPEG format. This transition will take a long time, but if you have an R7 camera, you can start creating images in HEIF. When you enable HDR Shooting with the HDR PQ Settings in the Shooting 2 menu, the Image Quality menu will show HEIF instead of JPEG. You can also convert HEIF to JPEG in the Playback 3 menu, making it compatible with applications that can't handle HEIF yet. I'll explain more about HDR PQ Settings and HEIF to JPEG conversion later in this chapter.

JPEG/HEIF vs. RAW

RAW files are like the initial information your camera captures but are untouched. Just as the film goes through processes in development, digital images also become a RAW file. Canon, for example, has a chip (DIGIC X) dedicated to this digital processing.

A RAW file is like a camera's developed negative. It holds all the info captured in high quality, without compression, sharpening, or special filters. The settings you used are saved, and when you convert the image, you can stick with them or make new choices using software like Adobe Camera Raw. It's similar to picking camera settings but done during editing.

RAW is like having the raw ingredients before cooking. It gives us all the details from the camera before it turns them into a standard image. While it takes more space than JPEG, RAW keeps all the original info in digital form, including camera settings.

Why not always use RAW? Many photographers prefer using a combination of RAW and JPEG/HEIF or just sticking to JPEG/HEIF. RAW files are great for detailed editing but can slow your workflow. If you need a good, untouched image, working with RAW takes more time – they take longer to save and need extra effort for post-processing, even if you use default settings or make small changes.

For those who want quick access to photos or take many pictures at once, using JPEG is better than RAW or HEIF. Wedding photographers, for instance, shoot thousands of photos, and they choose JPEG because it saves them time. They set up their camera beforehand to reduce the need for editing later. Since their JPEG photos turn out well due to their experience, there's usually no need to bother with RAW or deal with the complexities of HEIF early on.

JPEG was created to make image files smaller while keeping most information. It was made before modern digital cameras and was used to shrink files for sending over slow internet connections, especially for early digital SLRs with lower-resolution files.

JPEG and HEIF make image files smaller by removing some details, but JPEG is still popular because it allows different quality levels. The difference between the original file and the compressed versions might be hard to notice at the highest quality, making JPEG a good option.

I usually take photos in RAW and JPEG Fine formats, but I have not used HEIF much since my software doesn't fully support it. I carry multiple large memory cards, so running out of space is rarely a concern. If needed, I transfer photos to my laptop during trips. I switch to JPEG Fine for sports photography to capture more continuous shots quickly.

However, during my recent trip to Europe, I opted for only RAW to save space on my laptop for post-processing images for a travel book.

CHAPTER 5: CAPTURING VIDEO

Movie Shooting Menu

Movie Recording Size

This is the first option in the Movie 1 menu. Your camera has many recording settings, such as ultra-high resolution 4K video. I'll give more details about using these settings later in this chapter, but briefly, you can choose from the following options.

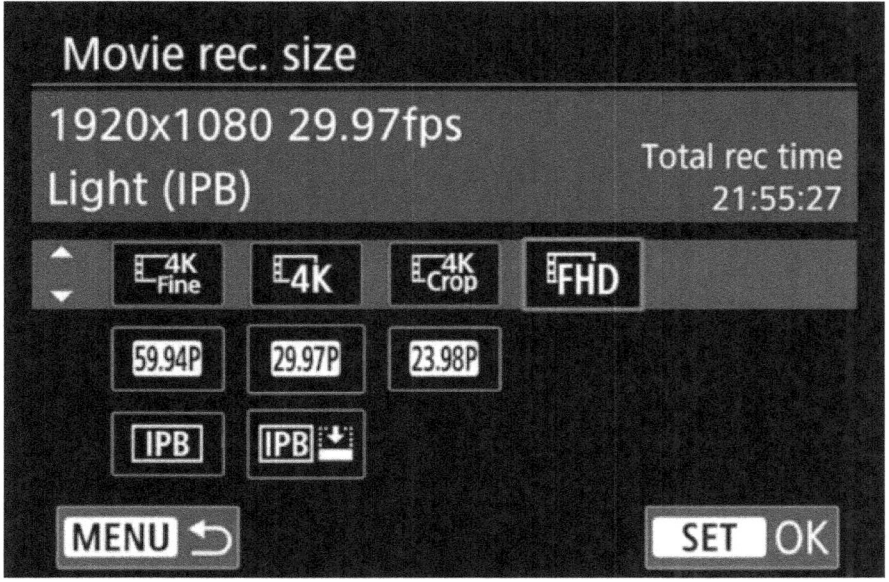

- **Image size:** This is about the movie's clarity – either super clear (4K) or regular clear (Full HD). The actual clarity and size of the movie can change based on how well it's recorded and some settings. Using the full camera sensor, the R7 camera can record clear videos in 4K (3840 × 2160) and regular clear videos in Full HD (1920 × 1080). It can also do a special 4K video with a closer view. You can use time-lapse modes for both super clear and regular clear videos.

- **Frame Rate:** This is how many pictures or parts of a video are taken each second. It's usually shown as 120, 60, 30, or 24 frames per second. In NTSC mode (used in North America, Japan, and other places), the actual rates are slightly different: 119.9, 59.94, 29.97, and 23.98 frames per second. In Europe and other countries, they often use 100, 50, and 25 frames per second.

Not every video speed works with every picture size. For instance, with NTSC, you can use 4K Fine with speeds of 29.97 and 23.98, and 4K Crop only works with a speed of 59.94. Standard 4K and FHD support speeds are 59.94, 29.97, and 23.98. High Frame Rate movies, which we'll talk about soon, record videos at 119.9 (NTSC) or 100.0 (PAL) but play them back more slowly.

- **Compression Method:** To make your videos take up less space and not strain your storage, each frame is compressed using IPB formats (or ALL-I for time-lapse videos).

All movies use the MP4 format as a "container" for video files, using the MPEG4 AVC/H.264 codec. MP4 is a widely supported international standard, and the files get a .MP4 extension.

High Frame Rate

When you turn on High Frame Rate for videos, your recording speed is faster (119.9 NTSC or 100.0 PAL), but when you watch it, it's slowed down (29.97/25.00 fps), making the action 4 times slower. If you use the HDMI port to show the video, it will be 2 times slower instead.

Remember, no sound is recorded, and clips can only be 1 hour and 30 minutes long. There might be flickering in certain lights, and ISO speeds are between 100 and 12800 (or 25600 with extended settings). Use a High Frame Rate for cool slow-motion scenes or to study movement in your videos.

Digital Zoom

If you set the Movie Size to FHD 29.97, 23.98 (NTSC), or 25 (PAL), you can use a digital zoom that magnifies up to 10 times. However, remember that this may reduce image quality and increase noise because it crops the image. To enable the zoom, tap the W/T icon or assign a key, like the ISO button, in the Custom Functions 3 menu. Once activated, use the up/down buttons to zoom in and out.

Sound Recording

You can pick Auto, Manual, or Disable in this setting. You also have the option to turn the wind filter and audio noise reduction on or off.

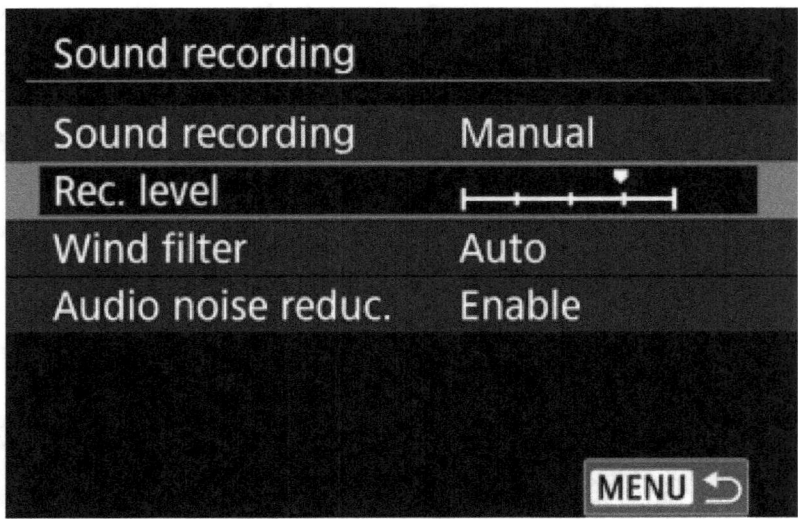

In Movie Scene Intelligent Auto (A+) mode, you can only choose On (Auto level) or Off, and you can't adjust the left/right balance.

- **Auto:** It adjusts the volume for you.

- **Manual:** Pick from 64 sound levels. Adjust the Rec Level and turn the QCD knob while looking at the decibel meter at the bottom of the screen. Aim for an average of -12 dB for loud sounds. Avoid reaching the 0 point on the far right to prevent distortion.

- **Disable:** Record your video quietly, then enhance it with voice, narration, music, or other sounds using your video editing software. Remember that if you're connected to an external device like an HDMI recorder, ensure sound recording is enabled on the camera to capture audio.

- **Wind Filter:** Turn off the option to lessen wind noise and minimize low tones in recordings. If wind isn't an issue, your audio quality will improve without this setting. For even better results, use an external microphone with a windshield.

- **Audio Noise Reduction:** This filter makes the clicking sounds from your camera lens quieter when it's focusing. Some lenses are louder, so only use them when needed since it can slightly affect the sound quality. It also helps reduce background noise. The "High" setting reduces noise but may impact sound quality more. Check your clips with headphones to decide if you need noise reduction, and you can adjust headphone noise in the Set-up 3 menu.

You can use the microphone on the camera for recording, but it's better to connect a stereo microphone to the camera's left side for improved results. Using an external microphone is recommended to avoid capturing camera sounds. If you want to monitor the audio, use headphones and adjust the volume in the Movie version of the Quick Controls menu.

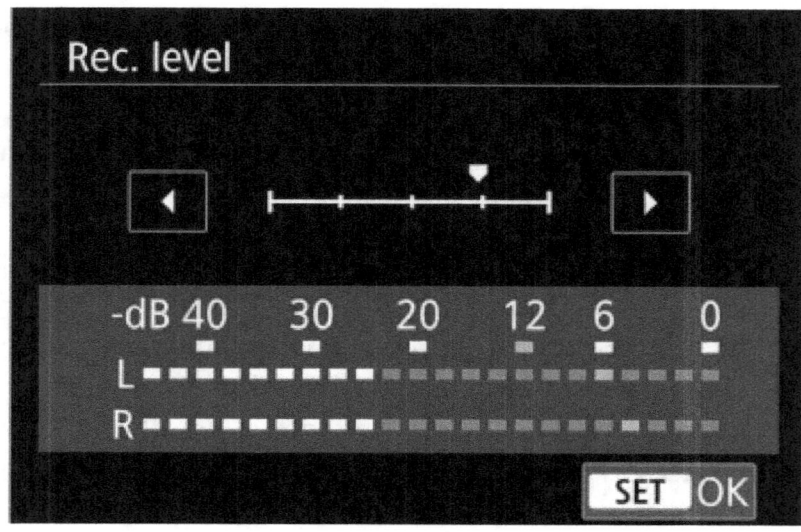

Movie ISO Speed Settings

This is the first option related to movies in the Movie Shooting 2 menu. It allows you to set ISO parameters for filming.

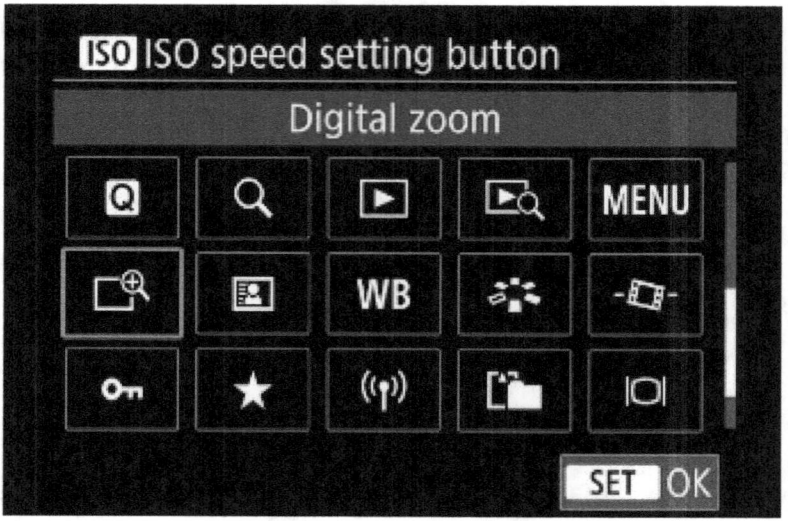

You can choose a specific ISO speed or set limits for the camera's automatic selection of ISO settings and shutter speeds.

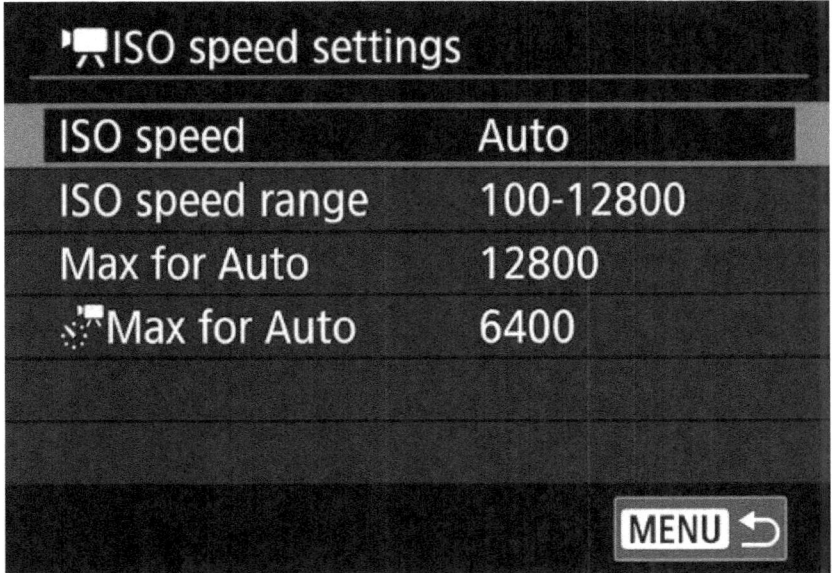

- **ISO Speed:** You can choose ISO speed in Manual mode, but it's automatic in other modes. In Movie Manual mode, you can pick ISO from 100 to 25600 or use Auto.

Using the Manual exposure mode with the Auto setting is like having a semi-automatic mode. You manually choose the aperture and shutter speed, and the camera automatically adjusts the ISO to get the correct exposure. It allows you to be creative with your videos by picking the aperture for focus control and still getting the right shutter speed for smooth footage.

- **ISO Speed Range:** You can choose the lowest and highest ISO settings.

  - **Minimum:** You can adjust the sensitivity settings of your camera from low (ISO 100) to high (ISO 12800), and there's also an extra high option (H) equivalent to ISO 25600.

    When you use Auto exposure with Canon Log, the lowest speed is ISO 400. You can manually choose ISO 100 and ISO 200, but they're called expanded L settings, and there might be some loss in quality.

  - **Maximum:** You can choose the highest ISO setting, up to ISO 25600. The Highlight Tone Priority setting doesn't impact this. It's handy to prevent accidentally selecting settings. For instance, I set ISO 1600 at concerts as the minimum and 6400 as the maximum. In daylight, I might limit ISO to 100 to 800.

- **Max for Auto:** This is like a safety backup for the highest setting in Auto ISO.

- **Time-lapse Max for Auto:** Choose the highest ISO setting for shooting 4K/Full HD time-lapse movies in different exposure modes. The default maximum is 12800, but you can choose between ISO 400 and 12800.

HDR Shooting

This option in the Movie Shooting 2 menu turns HDR movie recording on or off. It's different from the Shooting 2 option in Still photo mode, and you can choose to enable, turn on or off, or have both. No extra settings are needed. Remember that settings like Auto Slow Shutter, Canon Log, Clarity, and Creative Filters prevent HDR shooting.

Movie Av 1/8-stop Increments

RF-mount lenses give you more precise control over apertures compared to EF/EF-S lenses. Canon utilizes this by allowing adjustments in 1/8th stop increments, which is beneficial for maintaining consistent exposure, especially in movie shooting. This feature is available in Movie exposure modes (Av and M), where you have full aperture control. You can enable 1/8th-stop increments instead of the 1/2- or 1/3-stop jumps set in Custom Functions 1. Note that this feature doesn't work with EF or EF-S lenses.

Movie Auto Slow Shutter

This is the final movie option in the Movie Shooting 2 menu. It lets the camera automatically choose a slower shutter speed (not faster than 1/30th second) when filming in Program or Aperture-priority mode at a 60p frame rate. You can decide to turn this feature on or off, and I'll explain more about how frame rates impact your videos later in this chapter.

- **Disable:** Choose frame rates of 1/60th second or faster in Program and Av exposure modes for 60p video. It makes the video smoother, sharper, and more natural. But in low light, your video might look darker.

- **Enable:** Slower shutter speeds, like 1/30th second, make movies look brighter and less noisy using a lower ISO setting. But, moving things might appear blurry or leave a noticeable trail due to the longer exposure.

Canon Log Settings

C-log is a special setting in Movie Shooting 3 that helps capture more video details. It works by adjusting how the camera records light and color non-linearly. It creates a flat-looking, low-contrast video that might not look good initially but can be enhanced during editing using professional programs like DaVinci Resolve, Adobe Premiere Pro, or Apple Final Cut Pro. The goal is to preserve the original scene's dynamic range and make a rich, full-range video.

Canon Log settings

Canon Log	On (C.LOG3)
View Assist.	Off
Characteristics	0, 0, 0
Color space	BT.709

MENU ↩

Canon Log, which Canon Log3 now replaces, theoretically gives you a broader range of tones in your photos or videos, about 800 percent more or 12 f/stops, when using ISO 400 or higher. To capture extra detail, there's an ISO boost. Canon also added a "View Assist" feature in the Set-up menu, accessible from HDMI, allowing you to preview a corrected version in the camera before processing. Log profiles distribute captured data evenly across exposure stops, desaturating colors to avoid over-saturation and make corrective grading easier.

This book focuses more on camera features than the technical details of Canon Log technology. However, if you edit videos and adjust colors afterward, you might like the 10 "look-up tables" (LUTs) Canon offers. When viewing it on another screen, these tables help fix the gamma and color of your recorded video. You can download these helpful LUTs from Canon's website.

Canon Log 3 is an improved camera setting with benefits over the basic Canon Log. It doubles the base ISO to 800, capturing more highlights with one stop less exposure. It also avoids cutting off black values, giving better results in shadows when editing. Compared to Canon Log, C-Log3 provides a bit more dynamic range and improved shadows and works better with Canon's Cinema EOS models' look-up tables.

To film movies using Canon Log, do the following steps:

1. Switch to Manual exposure in Movie mode.

2. Go to Canon Log Settings in the Movie Shooting 3 menu.

3. Turn on Canon Log (C.Log3) for a broader dynamic range. To stop Canon Log recording, choose Off.

4. If needed, enable View Assist to see a clearer display on the camera's screen without affecting the video files.

5. Use easy sliders to Adjust video settings like Sharpness, Strength, Saturation, or Hue.

6. Pick either BT.709 or BT.2020 for HDMI color output – these define aspects like resolution and color for HD TV signals. If you know the difference, you're good to go.

7. Select ISO speed, shutter speed, and aperture settings.

8. Record your video onto the camera's memory card or an external recorder.

Time-lapse Movie

There are no movie options in the Movie Shooting 4 menu, so let's move on to the first one in Movie Shooting 5. Time-lapse photography is not only for nature lovers capturing flowers blooming; it's now widely used in movies and TV to show time passing like the sun moving across the sky or the changing seasons. Canon has made this technique accessible to you.

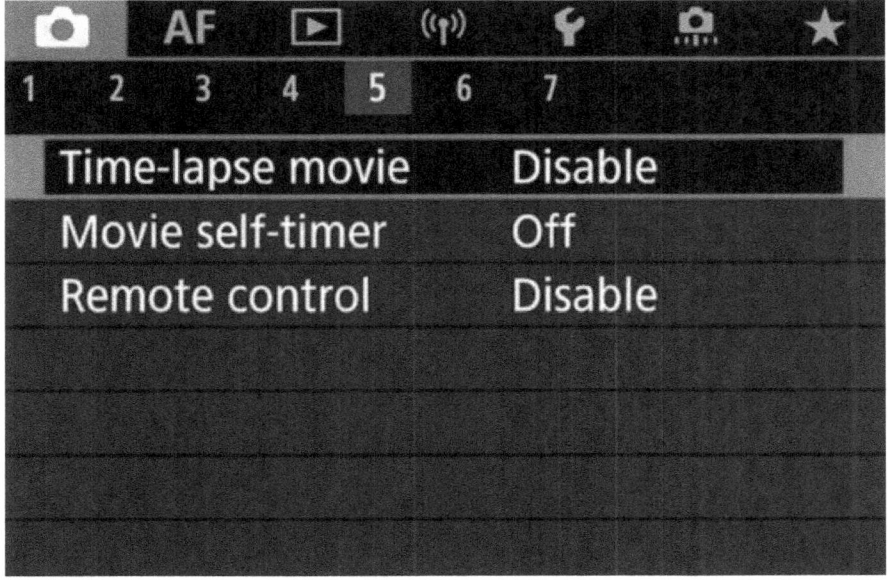

I'll quickly go over the main settings, and you can see the first five in the image below.

Time-lapse movie ⛏️ 📹FHD 29.97P IPB

Time-lapse	Enable
Interval	00:00:03
No. of shots	0300
Movie rec. size	FHD
Auto exposure	Fixed 1st frame

🎥 00:11:57   ▶ 00:00:15

MENU ↩

- **Time-lapse:** Click "Enable" to start setting up, or choose "Disable" to turn off this option.

- **Interval:** You can pick how much time passes between each shot, with a maximum interval of 99 hours, 59 minutes, and 59 seconds.

- **Number of shots:** Choose how many pictures you want to take, between 2 and 3,600. The app will tell you how long it will take. If the time is in red, it means your memory card might be too small or incorrectly formatted. Don't worry if you use an SDXC card; it's automatically formatted. Recording stops when the card is full or hits the maximum file size.

- **Movie Recording Size:** You can pick between high-quality video options: 4K at 29.97 frames per second

(NTSC) or 4K at 25.00 frames per second (PAL). Alternatively, you can choose Full HD at 29.97 frames per second (NTSC) or 25.00 per second (PAL). In all cases, ALL-I compression is applied.

- **Auto Exposure:** You have options:

  o **Fixed 1st Frame:** Metering measures light for the initial frame, setting the exposure, and maintains that same exposure for all following frames. It's handy for consistent exposure, even if the lighting conditions change.

  o **Each Frame:** For every picture taken in the time-lapse of a city skyline from morning to evening, the camera adjusts to the right brightness to match each part of the day.

- **Screen Auto Off:** Scroll down to find this and the next entry. You can keep the screen on for about 30 minutes by turning off automatic dismissal or enable it to turn off the screen 10 seconds after you start shooting, giving you time to check your framing and exposure.

- **Beeps per Image Taken:** Turn each photo's sound on or off using the electronic shutter for time-lapse movies.

Movie Self-timer

This cool feature lets you wait 10 or 2 seconds before recording a video. Choose 10 seconds if you need time to get ready, like fixing your hair, or choose 2 seconds if you're all set. It's handy if you don't have a remote control – it gives the camera a moment to steady after pressing the record button. (Tip: press gently, don't stab!)

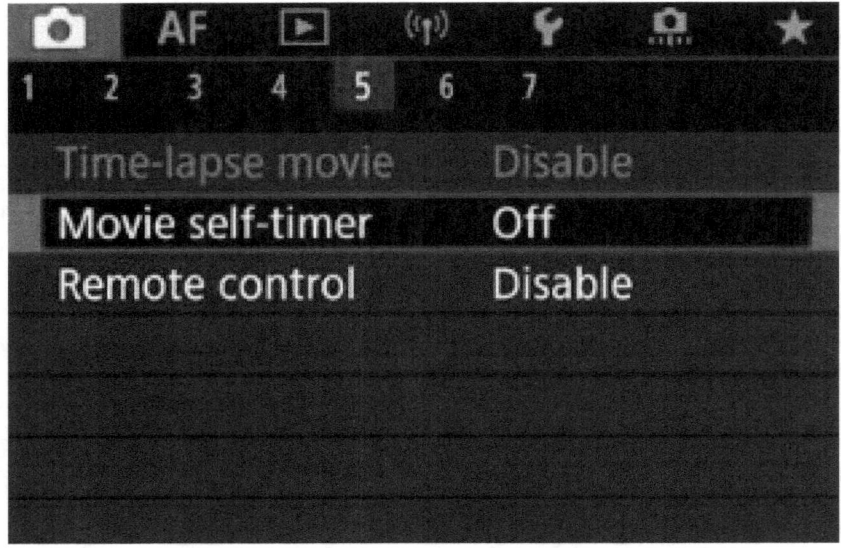

Vloggers might not need this feature for spontaneous sessions since those who use this camera are likely skilled at editing any rushed or awkward moments in their videos.

Remote Control

To use a remote control for starting or stopping movie recording, ensure your camera is set up to allow it. The R7 works with the Remote Controller RC-6 and Wireless Remote Control BR-E1. Check the manual with your remote to understand each device's features.

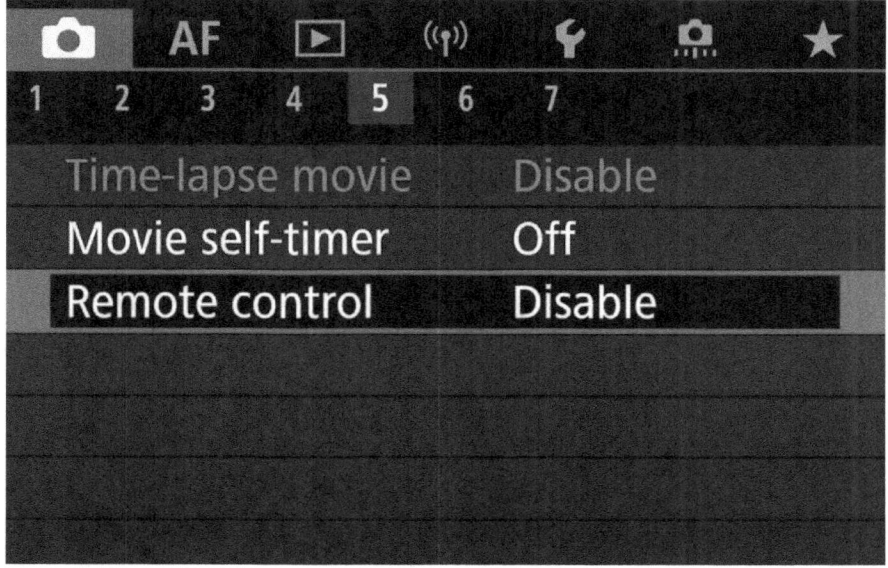

IS (Image Stabilizer Mode)

This is the first option in the Movie Shooting 6 menu. If your camera uses stabilization in certain lenses, it can also use electronic stabilization called Movie Digital IS when recording videos.

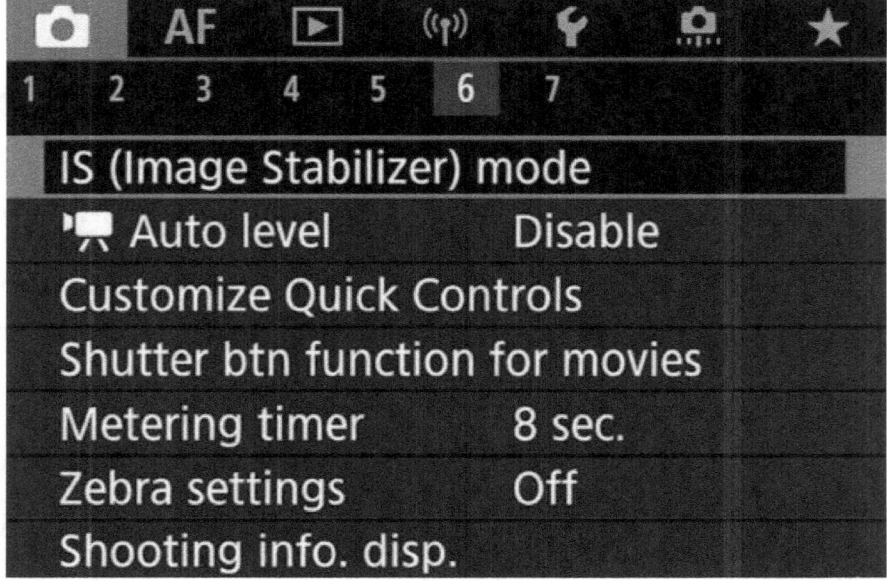

Movie digital image stabilization works by adjusting the video frames to counteract camera movement. It shifts the pixels within the frame to keep non-moving elements in the same position. This process may crop the edges of the frame, leading to a magnified final movie.

Movie Digital IS is great because it can be used with any lens you choose. It helps reduce shaking for lenses without built-in stabilization, and if your lens already has stabilization, Movie Digital IS teams up with it and the camera's stabilization for even better results.

Use this special camera feature along with the stabilization of your lenses. If your lens has stabilization, make sure it's turned on – the camera will remind you if it's off. Canon has a list of lenses with digital and optical image stabilization. Note that

Movie IS won't work with lenses longer than 800mm or with tilt/shift, fisheye, or third-party lenses.

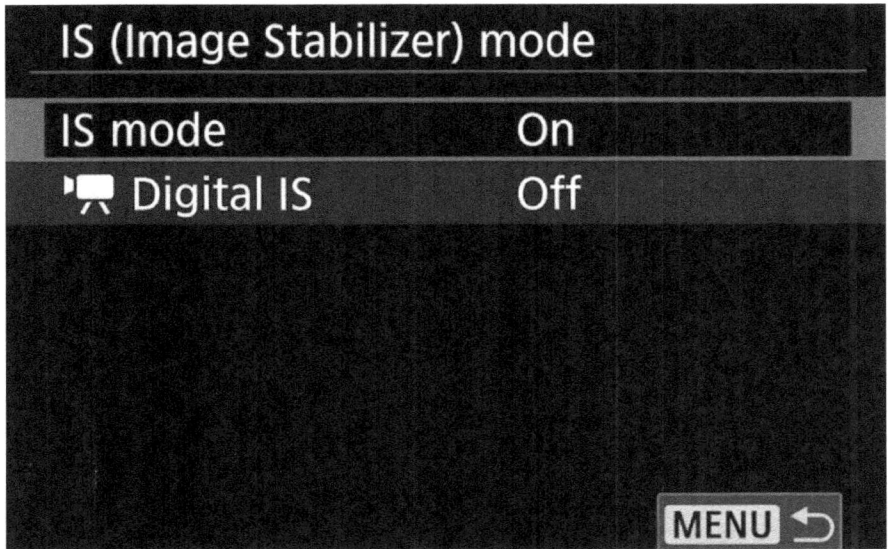

Here are your choices :

- **IS Mode (On, Off):** If your lens has no image stabilization, you'll see this choice. It lets you control whether the camera stabilizes images inside itself. Turn the camera off on a tripod to avoid unnecessary adjustments. Keep it on for handheld shooting.

- **Movie Digital IS (Off, On, Enhanced):** This choice shows whether your lens has image stabilization, and it's the only one available if your lens has IS.

    - **On:** This setting reduces shaky camera movement and slightly zooms in on the image, which is especially good for wide-angle lenses.

99

○ **Enhanced:** If the camera shakes a lot, this feature helps reduce it, but the image might look a bit blurry and noisy, so use it only when necessary.

Shutter Button Function for Movies

This setting lets you choose what the shutter button does while recording a video. It takes precedence over any Custom Functions 3 menu settings for button customization. You can set different actions for pressing the button halfway and fully pressing it.

- **Half-press:** You can pick :

  ○ **Metering plus Movie Servo AF:** Use the standard setting to start measuring light and focusing by pressing the shutter button when you want the camera to keep following and adjusting the focus on a moving subject.

  ○ **Metering plus One-Shot AF:** If you don't want the camera focus to keep changing, especially in still shots with only the camera moving, use the shutter release button to set and maintain focus on your main subject.

  ○ **Metering Only:** Select this option if you only want to use the shutter button to start metering

- **Fully-press:** You have the option to pick:

○ **Start/Stop Movie Recording:** This setting lets you use one button to begin or end recording videos by fully pressing the shutter release. It's handy to use the same button to take photos and record videos. Since you can't capture photos while recording videos, assigning the video function to the shutter release is a practical choice. But don't worry; you can still grab individual frames from your videos if you want a still shot.

○ **No function:** When it's set like this by default, pressing hard doesn't do anything.

Zebra Settings

This tool warns you if the bright parts of your image are brighter than what you set. It's like the blinking highlights on digital cameras, but it's better because it alerts you before taking the photo, letting you decide how bright it is. Professionals often use this feature in video shooting, measured in IRE, which stands for Institute of Radio Engineers.

Zebra settings

Zebra	On
Zebra pattern	Zebra 1+2
Zebra 1 level	5±5%
Zebra 2 level	50%

MENU ↰

To use Zebra pattern warnings, go to the menu, pick a pattern, and set the brightness between 5 and 100 (depending on the pattern). After seeing the results on your screen, adjust your exposure settings to make highlights less bright.

How bright is too bright? If your image shows a Zebra pattern at 100 IRE, it's overexposed – pure white with lost details. Keep facial tones around 70 to 90 IRE; Caucasian skin is usually around 80, darker tones around 70, and lighter areas near 90— Set Zebra pattern sensitivity to avoid overexposure, indicated by flashing stripes on your display. The pattern doesn't appear in your final image; it's a tool to prevent overexposure. Maximum brightness varies based on camera settings like Canon Log, Highlight Tone Priority, Picture Style, and HDR-PQ.

Your changes consist of:

- **Zebra:** Pick On to show Zebra patterns while filming, or choose Off to hide them.

- **Zebra Pattern:** You can pick between two Zebra patterns: lines slanting to the right or left, appearing over bright areas. You can also choose Zebra 1+2, showing a mix of both patterns to identify areas with a combination of brightness levels.

- **Zebra 1 Level:** You can adjust the Zebra 1 display between 5% and 95%, with a plus or minus 5% tolerance.

- **Zebra 2 Level:** You can choose the Zebra 2 level anywhere between 50 to 100 percent.

Reverse Display

This is the first choice in the Shooting 7 menu. Suppose the automatic white balance or any of the seven preset settings (Auto, Daylight, Shade, Cloudy, Tungsten, White Fluorescent, or Flash) don't work for you. In that case, you can customize the white balance using the Custom menu or a specific color temperature value.

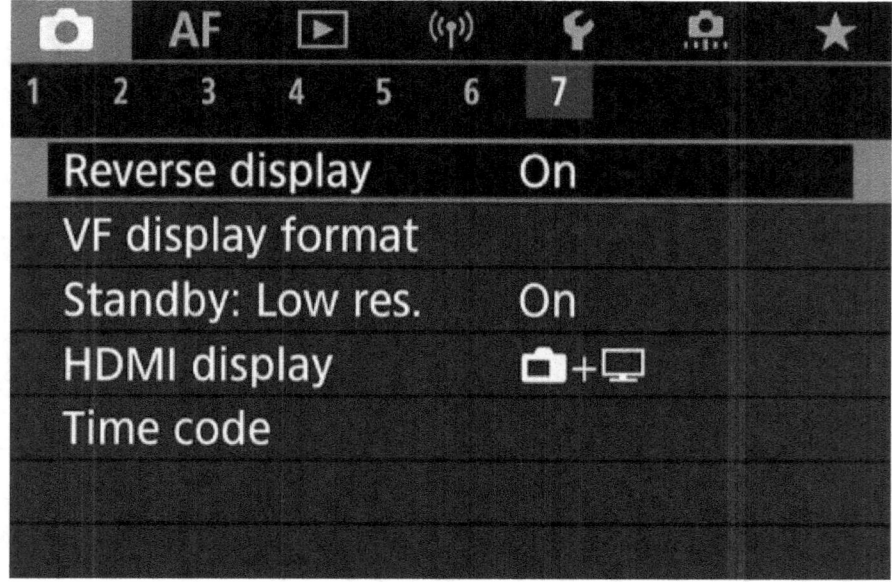

Standby: Low Resolution

Imagine this setting as a way to prevent your camera from getting too hot and damaging itself. When you're previewing or recording video in 4K at high speeds, it generates a lot of heat. This control helps by showing a lower-quality preview to reduce the camera's temperature and save power. It's beneficial to keep the camera on standby for extended periods. While on standby, the image quality isn't crucial, and it helps the camera stay cool and use less power.

If you use Digital Zoom, you can't use this setting. If you're not worried about overheating, change it from the default On to Off. It will make your camera respond faster when you start retaking pictures and show a better display on the standby screen.

HDMI Display

When sending video to another device, you can decide if it shows on both your camera and the external device or just on the external recorder or monitor.

- **Camera+External:** When using the HDMI mode, the camera and another device connected via HDMI will display the movie. However, you can't record to the camera's memory card in this mode. The HDMI display only shows the video without additional information and is primarily used for viewing menus and playback. The camera shows the live video with overlays when capturing, but menus and playback are not displayed on the camera screen. This mode helps monitor your recording on both the camera and the HDMI device, especially if a long cable connects them.

- **External Only:** The camera won't display any video, info, menus, or playback image – only the external device will show them.

Time Code

Video experts appreciate having time codes in their files because they act like precise markers, showing a video's hours, minutes, seconds, and frames. It helps with editing by allowing easy identification and synchronization of frames and audio.

Time code

Count up	Rec run
Start time setting	
Movie rec count	Rec time
Movie play count	Rec time
HDMI	
Drop frame	Enable

MENU ↩

The time code system also accounts for variations in frame rates, ensuring accurate matching with actual time intervals. Although I won't delve deeply into technical aspects like time codes in this book, you don't need a basic introduction if you're already using them.

The Time Code submenu offers various options for those familiar with this advanced feature.

- **Count Up:** Pick Rec Run if you want the timer to increase while recording the video. Choose Free Run (or Time of Day) if you want the timer to keep running even when not recording. It is helpful for syncing clips from multiple cameras shooting the same event. Free Run allows you to watch videos captured simultaneously during editing, even if the cameras record at different times. The time code will always be recorded in the movie file when Free Run is selected, except for HFR clips.

- **Start Time Setting:** Usually, the camera uses its clock to show the time when you're shooting, starting at 00 for each minute. This option lets you type in any time you want or reset it to 00:00:00:00.

- **Movie Rec. Count:** Choose whether you want to see how much time has passed in the current video clip on the screen or the Time Code when recording the video.

- **Movie Play Count:** Choose whether you want to see how much time has passed in the current video clip on the screen or the Time Code when recording the video.

- **HDMI:** Choose "Enable" to include the time code in the HDMI video output, or select "Disable" to exclude it. When "Enable" is chosen for the Record Command output, the camera's Start/Stop action syncs with the external recording device. If "Disable" is selected, the external recording device controls the starting and stopping actions.

- **Drop Frame:** If you pick 30 fps, you get 29.97 frames per second, 60 fps gives you 59.95 frames, and HFR is 119.9 fps. It causes a difference between recorded time and time code. Turning on "Enable" makes the camera skip some time code numbers to fix this discrepancy. If disabled, you might see a few seconds difference per hour.

Movie Autofocus Menus

When you choose a movie shooting mode, you'll see six new menus for Movie Autofocus with 19 options. Some entries are the same as those in still shooting. I'll talk about three new entries related to autofocus for shooting movies. Your other movie autofocus settings, like AF Method, will be similar to what you're used to in still shooting.

Movie Servo AF

With the R7, this feature works like Continuous AF. When turned on, it uses Movie Servo AF. If turned off, you can autofocus by half-pressing the shutter or using the AF-ON button. When on, the focus adjusts constantly without pressing the shutter halfway.

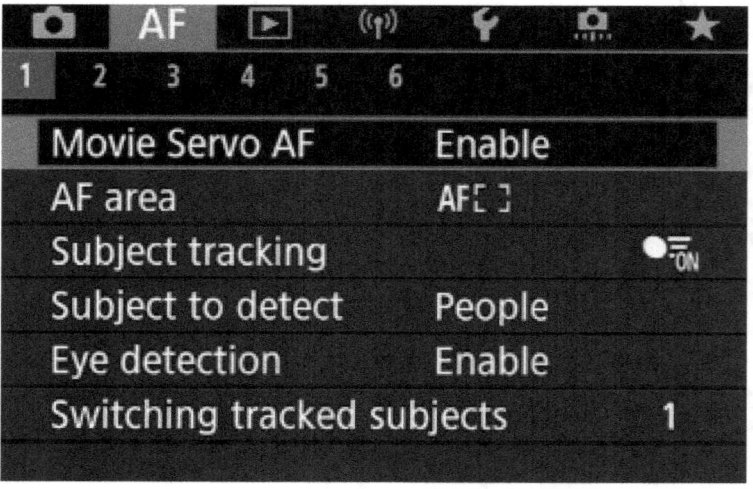

To lock focus or pause, tap the Servo AF icon on the lower left of the LCD screen. Tap again to resume. Movie Servo AF restarts if you press MENU, Playback, or change the AF method. You can set the camera's response with Movie Servo AF Speed.

Movie Servo AF Speed

You can make this choice if Movie Servo AF is turned on. It also works with lenses made after 2009 with USM or STM motors.

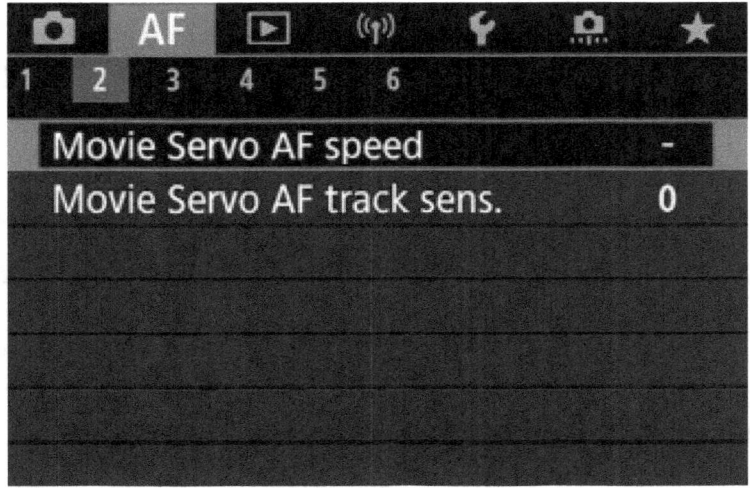

Here are your options:

- **When Active:** Always On makes the autofocus adjustment speed active before and during video shooting. During Shooting, AF activates speed adjustment only while you're recording video.

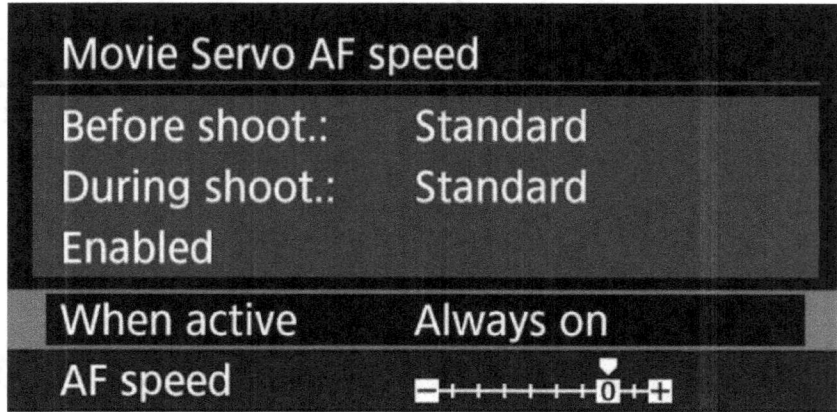

- **AF Speed:** Tap on the option and press Q/SET. After that, you can change the AF speed using the touch screen, QCD, or directional controls. Move the slider to set it from Slow (-7 to 0) to Standard (0) to Fast (+1 to +2).

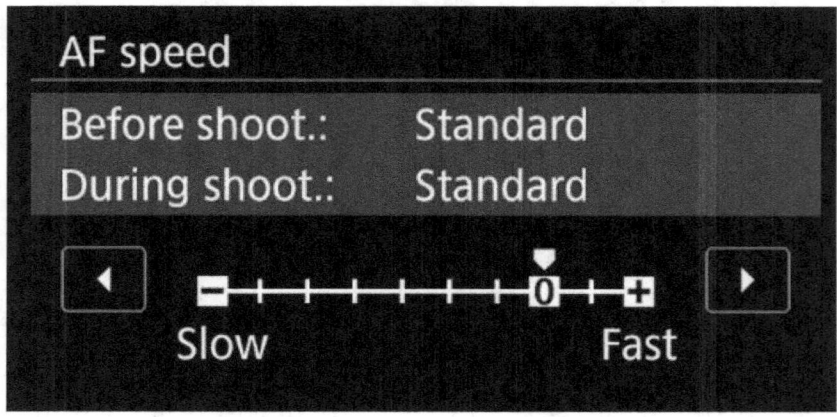

Movie Servo AF Tracking Sensitivity

Choose how fast the Movie Servo AF follows a moving subject by adjusting the Tracking Sensitivity in the Autofocus settings.

It's like adjusting the sensitivity in still photos but for videos. It can be handy when something moves in front of your main subject or when you're panning the camera. You can slide the scale from Locked On (slow) to Responsive (fast) or keep it standard at 0.

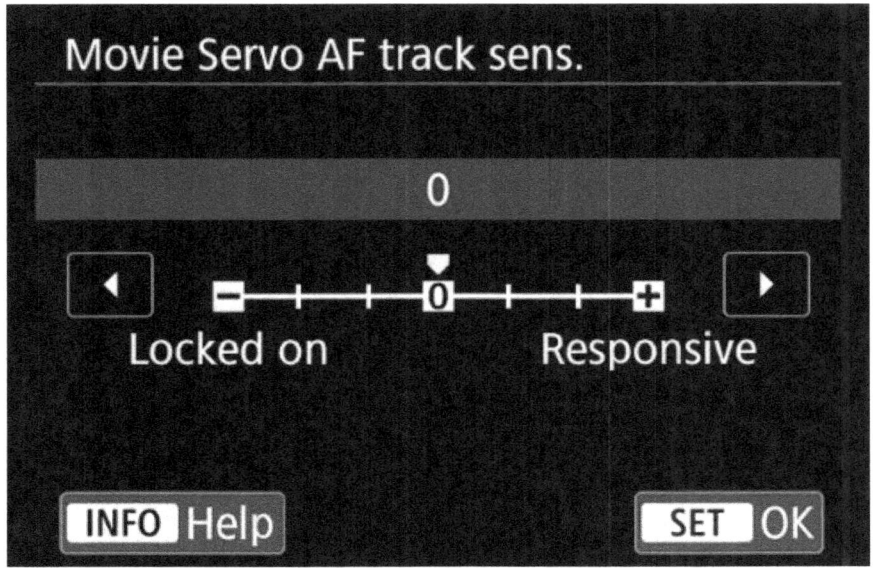

Locked On means the camera stays focused on the current subject, like a referee in a football game or someone in a city. Responsive settings make the camera follow a subject at the focus point, whether the same one is coming closer quickly or a new one is appearing.

CONCLUSION

You've reached the end of this guide, but your EOS R7 journey is just taking off. This camera isn't just a bunch of tech jargon; it's a powerful tool waiting to help you capture amazing photos in any situation.

Think of this guide as your launchpad. It's given you the basic knowledge to navigate the R7's features, but now it's time to ditch the manual and embrace the real magic of photography: taking great pictures.

So, whether you're scaling mountains, freezing sports action, or capturing wildlife on the move, the R7 is your trusty ally. It's built to handle whatever you throw at it and help you tell stories that go beyond ordinary snapshots.